Media Consolidation

Other Books of Related Interest

Opposing Viewpoints Series

Capitalism
The Corporatization of America
Digital Rights and Privacy

At Issue Series

Is America a Democracy or an Oligarchy?
Media Bias and the Role of the Press
The Media's Influence on Society

Current Controversies Series

Big Tech and Democracy
Freedom of the Press
Media Trustworthiness

"Congress shall make no law … abridging the freedom of speech, or of the press."

First Amendment to the U.S. Constitution

The basic foundation of our democracy is the First Amendment guarantee of freedom of expression. The Opposing Viewpoints series is dedicated to the concept of this basic freedom and the idea that it is more important to practice it than to enshrine it.

Media Consolidation

Avery Elizabeth Hurt, Book Editor

Published in 2024 by Greenhaven Publishing, LLC
2544 Clinton Street,
Buffalo NY 14224

Copyright © 2024 by Greenhaven Publishing, LLC

First Edition

All rights reserved. No part of this book may be reproduced in any form
without permission in writing from the publisher, except by a reviewer.

Articles in Greenhaven Publishing anthologies are often edited for length to meet page
requirements. In addition, original titles of these works are changed to clearly present
the main thesis and to explicitly indicate the author's opinion. Every effort is made to
ensure that Greenhaven Publishing accurately reflects the original intent of the authors.
Every effort has been made to trace the owners of the copyrighted material.

Cover image: Proxima Studio/Shutterstock.com

Library of Congress CataloginginPublication Data

Names: Hurt, Avery Elizabeth, editor.
Title: Media consolidation / Avery Elizabeth Hurt, book editor.
Description: Buffalo : Greenhaven Publishing, 2024. | Series: Opposing
  viewpoints | Includes bibliographical references and index. | Audience:
  Grades 10-12
Identifiers: LCCN 2024008272 | ISBN 9781534509689 (library binding) | ISBN
  9781534509672 (paperback)
Subjects: LCSH: Mass media--Mergers--Juvenile literature.
Classification: LCC P96.M46 M425 2024 | DDC 302.23--dc23/eng/20230318
LC record available at https://lccn.loc.gov/2024008272

Manufactured in the United States of America

Website: http://greenhavenpublishing.com

Contents

The Importance of Opposing Viewpoints	**11**
Introduction	**14**

Chapter 1: Does Media Consolidation Harm Democracy?

Chapter Preface	**18**
1. Local News and Civic Engagement Go Hand in Hand *Michael Barthel, Jesse Holcomb, Jessica Mahone, and Amy Mitchell*	**19**
2. Efforts to Increase Trust in Media Are Reaching the Wrong People *Rick Edmonds*	**25**
3. Corporate Media Distorts News in Harmful Ways *Andy Lee Roth and Steve Macek*	**31**
4. Corporations Shape Politics, and the Media Often Can't Stop It *Richard A. Devine and Michael Holmes*	**38**
5. News Organizations Need to Do More to Combat Misinformation *Jeffrey Gottfried, Amy Mitchell, Mark Jurkowitz, and Jacob Liedke*	**44**
6. Media Consolidation Allows Corporations to Control the Information that Americans Can Access *Margot Susca*	**48**
Periodical and Internet Sources Bibliography	**54**

Chapter 2: Does Media Consolidation Negatively Impact Culture?

Chapter Preface	**57**
1. Mergers and Consolidations Are Reshaping TV and Film Industries *Terry Gross*	**58**

2. Small and Medium Publishers Aren't Ready for the New Business Model 64
   Mike Harman

3. The Drive for Profit Is Causing Companies to Use AI to Replace Human Creators, but the Humans Are Fighting Back 70
   Brian Merchant

4. How Mass Media Impacts Culture 77
   Mark Poepsel

5. Netflix Can Use Its Media Power to Help Create Cross-Cultural Understanding 89
   Paolo Sigismondi

Periodical and Internet Sources Bibliography 93

Chapter 3: Does Media Consolidation Damage the Economy?

Chapter Preface 96

1. Turning News Divisions into Profit Centers Is a Bad Idea 97
   Margot Susca

2. Monopolies May Not Be All Bad 104
   Áine Doris

3. The Impact of Consolidation on TV Economics: It's Complicated 108
   Deborah Potter and Katerina Eva Matsa

4. Monopolies Have Both Advantages and Disadvantages 115
   Tejvan Pettinger

Periodical and Internet Sources Bibliography

121

Chapter 4: Does Media Consolidation Increase Misinformation, Bias, and Polarization?

Chapter Preface	**124**
1. Local Journalists Resist Corporate Push to Run Biased Content *Lisa Marshall*	**125**
2. The FCC Could Make Changes that Would Improve Local Coverage *Gregory J. Martin and Joshua McCrain*	**129**
3. Local News Helps Prevent Polarization and Nationalization *Matt Grossman*	**135**
4. Why We Need Media Diversity *Tim Dwyer*	**158**
Periodical and Internet Sources Bibliography	**163**
For Further Discussion	**165**
Organizations to Contact	**167**
Bibliography of Books	**171**
Index	**173**

| 10

The Importance of Opposing Viewpoints

Perhaps every generation experiences a period in time in which the populace seems especially polarized, starkly divided on the important issues of the day and gravitating toward the far ends of the political spectrum and away from a consensus-facilitating middle ground. The world that today's students are growing up in and that they will soon enter into as active and engaged citizens is deeply fragmented in just this way. Issues relating to terrorism, immigration, women's rights, minority rights, race relations, health care, taxation, wealth and poverty, the environment, policing, military intervention, the proper role of government—in some ways, perennial issues that are freshly and uniquely urgent and vital with each new generation—are currently roiling the world.

If we are to foster a knowledgeable, responsible, active, and engaged citizenry among today's youth, we must provide them with the intellectual, interpretive, and critical-thinking tools and experience necessary to make sense of the world around them and of the all-important debates and arguments that inform it. After all, the outcome of these debates will in large measure determine the future course, prospects, and outcomes of the world and its peoples, particularly its youth. If they are to become successful members of society and productive and informed citizens, students need to learn how to evaluate the strengths and weaknesses of someone else's arguments, how to sift fact from opinion and fallacy, and how to test the relative merits and validity of their own opinions against the known facts and the best possible available information. The landmark series Opposing Viewpoints has been providing students with just such critical-thinking skills and exposure to the debates surrounding society's most urgent contemporary issues for many years, and it continues to serve this essential role with undiminished commitment, care, and rigor.

The key to the series's success in achieving its goal of sharpening students' critical-thinking and analytic skills resides in its title—

Media Consolidation

Opposing Viewpoints. In every intriguing, compelling, and engaging volume of this series, readers are presented with the widest possible spectrum of distinct viewpoints, expert opinions, and informed argumentation and commentary, supplied by some of today's leading academics, thinkers, analysts, politicians, policy makers, economists, activists, change agents, and advocates. Every opinion and argument anthologized here is presented objectively and accorded respect. There is no editorializing in any introductory text or in the arrangement and order of the pieces. No piece is included as a "straw man," an easy ideological target for cheap point-scoring. As wide and inclusive a range of viewpoints as possible is offered, with no privileging of one particular political ideology or cultural perspective over another. It is left to each individual reader to evaluate the relative merits of each argument— as they see it, and with the use of ever-growing critical-thinking skills—and grapple with their own assumptions, beliefs, and perspectives to determine how convincing or successful any given argument is and how the reader's own stance on the issue may be modified or altered in response to it.

This process is facilitated and supported by volume, chapter, and selection introductions that provide readers with the essential context they need to begin engaging with the spotlighted issues, with the debates surrounding them, and with their own perhaps shifting or nascent opinions on them. In addition, guided reading and discussion questions encourage readers to determine the authors' point of view and purpose, interrogate and analyze the various arguments and their rhetoric and structure, evaluate the arguments' strengths and weaknesses, test their claims against available facts and evidence, judge the validity of the reasoning, and bring into clearer, sharper focus the reader's own beliefs and conclusions and how they may differ from or align with those in the collection or those of their classmates.

Research has shown that reading comprehension skills improve dramatically when students are provided with compelling, intriguing, and relevant "discussable" texts. The subject matter of

The Importance of Opposing Viewpoints

these collections could not be more compelling, intriguing, or urgently relevant to today's students and the world they are poised to inherit. The anthologized articles and the reading and discussion questions that are included with them also provide the basis for stimulating, lively, and passionate classroom debates. Students who are compelled to anticipate objections to their own argument and identify the flaws in those of an opponent read more carefully, think more critically, and steep themselves in relevant context, facts, and information more thoroughly. In short, using discussable text of the kind provided by every single volume in the Opposing Viewpoints series encourages close reading, facilitates reading comprehension, fosters research, strengthens critical thinking, and greatly enlivens and energizes classroom discussion and participation. The entire learning process is deepened, extended, and strengthened.

For all of these reasons, Opposing Viewpoints continues to be exactly the right resource at exactly the right time—when we most need to provide readers with the critical-thinking tools and skills that will not only serve them well in school but also in their careers and their daily lives as decision-making family members, community members, and citizens. This series encourages respectful engagement with and analysis of opposing viewpoints and fosters a resulting increase in the strength and rigor of one's own opinions and stances. As such, it helps make readers "future ready," and that readiness will pay rich dividends for the readers themselves, for the citizenry, for our society, and for the world at large.

Introduction

> *"The widest possible dissemination of information from diverse and antagonistic sources is essential to the welfare of the public."*
>
> *—Former Supreme Court justice Hugo Black*

For many years, the U.S. government made an effort to ensure that media served the public. Regulations prevented a single corporation from owning several newspapers or television stations in one area. It also kept any one station from reaching too large an audience. The idea was that viewers and listeners would be able to get a wide variety of diverse views and not be bombarded with messages from a single source. The intention was to strengthen democracy.

This all began to change in the 1980s during the administration of U.S. president Ronald Reagan. Deregulation—reducing the rules placed on industries—became very popular. Among other changes, Reagan abolished the Fairness Doctrine that had been issued in 1949 by the Federal Communications Commission (FCC), the agency that regulates the use of public airwaves. This rule required that in order to get a license to broadcast over public airways, a media outlet had to give equal time to all sides of controversial issues.

Deregulation continued when President Bill Clinton signed the Telecommunications Act of 1996. This piece of legislation greatly increased the limits on how many television stations and newspapers a single corporation could own. Then in 2017, the Federal Communications Commission abolished a longstanding policy that required news broadcasters to be based in their local communities.

During these decades there was also a weakening of antitrust laws and a shift toward less enforcement of them. Businesses were allowed to buy up other businesses and control markets. This made it difficult to prevent media consolidation. In 1983, 90 percent of U.S. media was controlled by fifty different companies. By 2017, 90 percent of U.S. media outlets were owned by only five companies.

In this book, authors from many different backgrounds address the complex issue of media consolidation. They look carefully at the benefits as well as the harms that occur when media is controlled by a few big companies. They examine the consequences of this trend and in some cases offer potential solutions to the problems they find.

In Chapter 1, the viewpoints focus on democracy. A free press is one of the pillars of democracy. Has media consolidation reduced the power of the press? Has media consolidation damaged democracy? The authors here agree that media consolidation has reduced the amount of local news coverage. But they do not all agree on whether control by a national corporation has resulted in more bias in news. Even when the corporations attempt to push their views, sometimes local journalists push back.

The authors in Chapter 2 look at the effect of media consolidation on culture. How has this trend affected television, film, and books? In this chapter, you'll learn about how digital publishing has changed the book market and why writers and actors went on strike. You will also learn about some of the potentially positive cultural impacts of media consolidation.

Chapter 3 offers a wide variety of viewpoints on the economics of media consolidation, particularly its impact on local economies and jobs. These authors argue that in some cases consolidation can increase prices, while in others they provide savings. But they all agree that when big companies buy out smaller media, workers lose their jobs.

Media Consolidation

The last chapter examines issues of utmost importance today: bias, misinformation, and polarization. Has media consolidation contributed to these problems? In this chapter, you'll read about the effects of this consolidation on newspapers and television news.

The concentration of media in the hands of a few powerful companies is a serious and complex problem. As the viewpoints in *Opposing Viewpoints: Media Consolidation* show, thoughtful people have nuanced views on the issues as well as a few ideas about how to address the potential problems caused by media consolidation.

CHAPTER 1

| Does Media Consolidation Harm Democracy?

Chapter Preface

Corporate consolidation and monopolies are taking over most industries. A few airlines grab almost all of the market; PepsiCo and Coca-Cola dominate the soft drink industry; a handful of corporations are behind most of the products in your local supermarket. And increasingly, the media is being gobbled up by a few giant corporations. While lack of competition poses problems in most industries, when the media is the victim of corporate consolidation, the problems are unique. Those problems may even include a danger to democracy. In this chapter, the authors look at media consolidation's effects on democracy at both local and national levels. While most authors here agree that consolidation is a problem for the media, they look at the issue from different perspectives.

The first viewpoint delves into the importance of local news to civic engagement—a key element of democracy. The founders of the United States of America knew that a free press is one of the essential pillars of democracy. However, their writings offer no suggestions about how that press should be supported. The author of another viewpoint takes on a crucial but thorny problem: the role of money in politics and media. Keeping the media free of the influence of both money and government is a challenge. Other authors discuss trust in media and offer advice and suggestions for how media outlets can address the increasing lack of trust.

| 18

VIEWPOINT 1

> *"The seven-in-ten Americans who say they live in areas with differing political views display very similar local news habits as those who believe most people in their communities share the same political views."*

Local News and Civic Engagement Go Hand in Hand

Michael Barthel, Jesse Holcomb, Jessica Mahone, and Amy Mitchell

In this viewpoint, the authors take a close look at the relationship between civic engagement and local news. It examines the results of a study by the Pew Research Center on civic engagement. The results of the study suggest that people who consume more local news are more connected to their communities, vote in elections, pay attention to local issues, and turn to multiple sources when researching these issues. When this viewpoint was originally published, Michael Barthel, Jesse Holcomb, Jessica Mahone, and Amy Mitchell were researchers at the Pew Research Center.

"Civic Engagement Strongly Tied to Local News Habits," by Michael Barthel, Jesse Holcomb, Jessica Mahone, and Amy Mitchell, Pew Research Center, November 3, 2016.

Media Consolidation

As you read, consider the following questions:

1. What does it mean to be civically engaged, according to this viewpoint?
2. Does the viewpoint suggest whether local news causes people to be more civically engaged? Why or why not?
3. What did the data cited in this viewpoint suggest about the local news habits of young people?

In local communities, the civically engaged – the people who vote, volunteer and connect with those around them – play a key role in community life. Thus, how and to what degree they stay informed about their communities carries added weight.

A new study by Pew Research Center in association with the John S. and James L. Knight Foundation reveals that, overall, the civically engaged are indeed more likely than the less engaged to use and value local news. But two particular aspects of civic engagement stand out as most closely associated with local news habits: a strong connection to one's community and always voting in local elections. Americans with one of these two attributes, the study finds, consistently display stronger local news habits across a range of measures: news interest, news intake (the number and types of sources they turn to) and news attitudes – their views of local news organizations.

This report focuses on five ways the public can connect to civic life and compares the local news habits of Americans who engage in each with those who do not. While these civic factors and news habits are related to each other, the data do not indicate the extent to which there is a causal relationship. In other words, the study does not point to whether civic engagement triggers local news interest, intake or more positive attitudes about local news media, or whether it is, in fact, the reverse.

The roughly one-in-five U.S. adults (19%) who feel highly attached to their communities demonstrate much stronger ties to local news than those who do not feel attached – revealing

| 20

Does Media Consolidation Harm Democracy?

a link between personal connection to these areas and a desire to stay more informed about current issues and events. Nearly six-in-ten (59%) of the highly attached follow local news very closely – about twice the share of the unattached (27%). Fully 44% regularly get community news from three or more different source types, compared with 17% of the unattached. And about a third (35%) think their local media do a good job of keeping them informed – more than double the share of the unattached (13%).

Similar to the highly attached, those who say they always vote in local elections (27% of U.S. adults) display strikingly stronger local news habits than those who do not regularly vote in local elections, perhaps a reflection of the unique service local journalism provides in its coverage of local elections and politics. They are more likely to follow local news closely (52% of regular local voters, compared to 31% of those who do not always vote), get local news from three or more source types (38% compared with 25%), follow multiple locally relevant topics (45% compared with 23%), and to approve of the job local news organizations do (27% compared with 18%).

Unlike local voting, however, regularly voting in national elections alone does not relate to stronger local news habits. Those who vote regularly in national elections – but not local elections – match those who do not vote regularly in *either* local or national elections in their more limited enthusiasm for local news.

While there is some overlap between those who are highly attached to their communities and regular local voters, these are largely separate groups: Only about a third (32%) of regular voters also consider themselves highly attached to their communities. And just under half (45%) of the highly attached are regular voters. Together, then, the two groups amount to 37% of U.S. adults – and these individuals discuss news more frequently than others, perhaps giving them greater influence on the public conversation about community affairs.

Another trait closely associated with broad community attachment is how well one knows their neighbors (23% of U.S. adults), which indeed reveals a similarly consistent connection

Media Consolidation

MEDIA GOES CORPORATE

In the earlier decades of the 20th century, there was a clear distinction between the corporates and the media houses with each existing in a symbiotic relationship with other.

[...]

However, things began to change from the 1970s onwards wherein the media houses started to resemble corporate entities both in the way they were managed and run and in the way they added spin to their stories.

It was no longer the case that media houses would criticize the corporates and still get advertising revenue. On the other hand, most media houses entered into partnerships with leading corporates wherein they published stories that were friendly to the advertisers.

The other parallel trend from this period to the present is that media houses became corporates themselves in the way they approached the business of news reporting.

Each media house aligned themselves to a particular corporate among the leading companies and thus, competition between the media houses ensured that the different groupings among industry in all countries could find sympathetic reporting from each media house.

[...]

Media houses were no longer the independent entities that they were earlier. This can be seen in the way media conglomerates like NewsCorp (owned by Rupert Murdoch) and other companies transformed themselves from being mere reporting of the news to agenda setting behavior.

[...]

In India, media conglomerates like the Times Group have risen in prominence in the last few decades thanks to the corporatization of the media. In the UK and the US, NewsCorp and Time Warner have come to symbolize big business and corporate media in all its glory.

The point here is that the media is no longer content with just reporting the news but instead, it has morphed into entities that set the agenda and entities that play a prominent role in shaping the public discourse.

In addition, the media houses entered into strategic partnerships with the leading corporates so that they get friendly press coverage.

> While the ethics of these trends can be debated, it is clear that media, the conception of what makes news has been altered, and the current media landscape is symbolic of corporatization of the industry.
>
> Finally, media houses in these times are not just purveyors of news but more importantly, they have become entities, which are solely concerned with making money.
>
> **"The Corporatization of the Media," by Prachi Juneja, Management Study Guide.**

to all three areas of local news habits. Fully half (52%) of those who know all their neighbors, for example, follow local news very closely, compared with 32% who don't know any of their neighbors. And 71% say the local media are in touch with their communities versus about half (49%) of those who don't know their neighbors.

U.S. adults who connect to civic life in other ways manifest stronger local news habits in some areas but not consistently across the board. The roughly one-quarter of Americans (27%) who actively participate in local groups and political activities, for example, demonstrate stronger news behaviors, but not more positive attitudes; just 22% approve of the job their local media are doing.

Americans who rate their local communities as excellent (29% of U.S. adults), on the other hand, have more positive views of their local news media than those who rate their communities less highly – about three-quarters of these high raters (77%) feel the local media are in touch with their local communities – but they express few stronger news habits.

The one civic factor studied here which seems to have the weakest connection to local news habits is the political diversity of one's community: The seven-in-ten Americans who say they live in areas with differing political views display very similar local news habits as those who believe most people in their communities share the same political views. While there are a few areas in which small differences emerge, roughly equal shares very closely follow

Media Consolidation

multiple locally relevant news topics and neighborhood news, consume local news via most source types, and approve of the job their local media are doing. What's more, this finding holds up when examined in terms of one measure of *observed* political diversity. Those who live in congressional districts where the 2012 presidential election was closely contested show similar local news habits to those living in districts that were not contested.

Those who are younger are generally less likely to be highly civically engaged than their elders, and as we have found in the past about news use in general, local news habits are less strong among younger adults. Nevertheless, the relationships we see between local news habits and these various aspects of civic engagement all hold up when controlling for age, as well as income and education.

These findings come from a study that asked U.S. adults a wide range of questions about their news habits and attitudes. The survey was conducted Jan. 12-Feb. 8, 2016, among 4,654 U.S. adults ages 18 and older who are members of Pew Research Center's nationally representative American Trends Panel.

VIEWPOINT

> "A Reuters survey report last summer found that trust levels are low worldwide and that the United States ranked last among 46 countries surveyed."

Efforts to Increase Trust in Media Are Reaching the Wrong People

Rick Edmonds

In this viewpoint, Rick Edmonds takes a look at the problems faced by journalism due to a decline in public trust of the media. Edmonds discusses the issue with several experts who offer opinions about what media outlets can do to improve the situation. The perspectives offered in this viewpoint suggest that finding ways to engage with readers and address their concerns is important to building trust for media outlets at both the local and national level. The viewpoint also indicates that focusing efforts on people who may not be overly informed about media—rather than those who are already loyal to the media outlet or those who are hostile to it—may be the best way to help get new subscriptions and allow media companies to survive, while also encouraging better media habits among the public. Rick Edmonds is media business analyst for the Poynter Institute, a nonprofit journalism school and research organization.

"Trust in media is low worldwide. Are media outlets reaching out to the wrong people?," by Rick Edmonds, The Poynter Institute, January 5, 2022. Reprinted by permission.

Media Consolidation

As you read, consider the following questions:

1. How, according to this viewpoint, might social media comments help newspapers address the problem of trust?
2. Why do the experts cited in this viewpoint recommend that media outlets be clear about their missions?
3. Why is it important that the public trust the media? What can the media do to earn this trust?

It has become an article of faith among editors and reporters that they need to come up with strategic efforts to build reader trust. However, a report late last year from the Reuters Institute for the Study of Journalism at the University of Oxford offers a sobering caution: Few efforts to build reader trust have reached beyond existing readers and likely subscribers to the truly skeptical.

I asked Rasmus Kleis Nielsen, director of the institute, whether this should be read as pessimism about the entire trust effort of the last several years. "I would say realism," he said. "Even if the truth is not entirely welcome ... we need to be clear-eyed about the incentives (at play)."

Right now, those incentives turn out to be foremost retaining subscribers or broadcast audiences, often paired with adding a new paid digital base, according to the report. That means "few individual news organizations have clear incentives for investing in building trust with indifferent, skeptical, or outright hostile parts of the public." In addition, few of the organizations with trust-building initiatives "can point to systematic efforts for tracking their effectiveness."

The conclusions were based on focus group conversations with journalists from four countries — the U.S., U.K., Brazil and India. (An earlier Reuters survey report last summer found that trust levels are low worldwide and that the United States ranked last among 46 countries surveyed).

On the one hand, Nielsen said, the principal measure of trust is the attitude of lay users alone. But he and co-author Benjamin

Toff thought it was worth digging deeper into how the trust challenge is playing out within news organizations. Given finite resources, it may make sense to individual organizations to focus engagement efforts narrowly on best prospects, the Reuters report authors write. The trouble is "for journalism more generally," they continue:

> If news outlets each focus on building trust with those already most likely to trust them — and many already compete for attention, trust, and reader revenue from the same, often already relatively trusting (and privileged) parts of the public — the people most indifferent to or distrusting towards news, who are most difficult to reach and most resistant to such appeals, and frankly often less commercially attractive, are at risk of being left behind or further alienated.

Editors in the discussions indicated awareness of the problem and offered some experimental solutions their organizations are trying.

Paul Volpe, who became editor of a new *New York Times* trust team in September, said the *Times* shares the Reuters perspective that there are groups of "hardcore loyalists who already believe you" and the "unconvertible who never will."

The *Times* is focusing on defining a third, middle group who might be those who do not yet know what to think: "Maybe it's a younger audience, maybe it's someone who's not exposed as much to media."

One avenue to defining that group, Volpe continued, may be social media comments, many of them based just on the incomplete picture a headline paints rather than an assessment of the whole story. Such posts may point the way to subsequent stories needed to address commenters' news concerns.

Suki Dardarian, senior managing editor and vice president of *The Star Tribune* in Minneapolis, offered a similar perspective from a regional newspaper: "If they're older, disinterested people, how hard do I have to work to get those people, when I have

Media Consolidation

a bunch of younger people coming in who might be more interested? Like, I'm not saying I'm writing them off, but you know, if I have to make some choices …"

She also spoke of *Star Tribune* initiatives considered successes in trust-building. Internal metrics suggested reader interest in uplifting stories so *The Star Tribune* has markedly upped its storytelling about faith, religion and spirituality.

Similarly an annual feature about lifestyle challenges, like cutting back on sugar or improving sleep, prompted the creation of a community format on those topics which has attracted thousands of comments.

For the toughest groups to reach, the report concludes that there are no easy answers, especially in a climate of polarization and media-bashing politicians. But it argues, "Much of the public sees journalism and news media as powerful institutions … and are unlikely to accept that the root of the problem lies elsewhere, or that they have few options at their disposal. Thus, giving up on building trust may look like a lack of real interest in the issue."

I asked Nielsen for further thoughts on what outlets might do. He offered three.

"Familiarity does not breed contempt, and that's quite encouraging," he said. Outlets should not be reticent to "show the value of their work."

Nielsen also thinks that outlets "should be as clear as possible about the mission of the organization," particularly in an era where large segments of the public suspect hidden agendas. "You need to have ideals. Say it and then show it."

Nielsen has noticed (as I have) how many of the best digital startups are explicit about their mission and editorial standards. Many newspapers, by contrast, "may be 100 years old, but it is easy to forget that, especially among a community of younger readers, what you stand for may not be known," he said.

Third, Nielsen suggests — as the report does — that outlets need to spend some time facing facts about what they think about alternate trust strategies. "No one can do everything," Nielsen said, but it has been easy to back into a narrow approach without much reflection.

He offered, as examples of creative approaches, a Canadian Broadcast Corporation initiative to embed journalists in pop-up newsrooms in remote Indigenous communities or the *Los Angeles Times'* "reckoning with its own history" of inadequately covering the many ethnic and racial groups it intends to serve.

Looking forward, Nielsen suggested that outlets could borrow a page from the playbook of successful politicians. "You do one set of things to energize the base and another to reach the undecideds."

His agenda for 2022 includes more academic work to understand the everyday impact of platforms and devising online experiments to see what's working among what's being tried.

I also asked for a reaction to the report from Joy Mayer, founder and director of Trusting News (and a Poynter adjunct faculty member). "It gets at some absolutely crucial tensions," she said. "There are choices to be made about who you want to serve."

Even if the goal ends up being just to seek a broader audience, she said, "you are going to encounter people who are hostile … and there are others who are misinformed or have reasons to be mistrustful."

Her 6-year-old project, co-sponsored by the Reynolds Institute at the University of Missouri and the American Press Institute, has embarked on a series of experiments under the banner of "the road to pluralism." It has been A-B testing, for instance — as the Reuters report recommends — whether explicit links to a mission statement make a given piece of content more credible.

The Reuters report notes that hostile assaults from some politicians on "the media," so prevalent here, are a huge issue also for the Brazilian and Indian editors who participated in the study. The level of hostility toward journalists and their organizations, together with echo chambers for animosity and misinformation, have induced a grim mood among many journalists, the report found.

Media Consolidation

It doesn't suggest any easy solution, but I would concur with the Reuters authors that this is no time to give up on identifying persuadable audience segments and a sustained effort to gain their trust. And for realism, as Nielsen suggested, about how far along outlets actually are.

VIEWPOINT 3

> "Corporate news media are guilty of both 'sins of omission' (neglecting significant facts about important issues, failing to follow up on stories that challenge the status quo) and 'sins of distortion' (framing news that contradicts conventional wisdom as "opinion," failing to interpret clearly interrelated events)."

Corporate Media Distorts News in Harmful Ways

Andy Lee Roth and Steve Macek

In this viewpoint, Andy Lee Roth and Steve Macek discuss Truthout's Project Censored, which is a nonprofit news watch that monitors the ways in which corporate media omits or distorts important news stories. By underreporting on or distorting these important news stories, corporate media harms the public by suggesting that a story is trivial and not worth discussing. The authors consider this to be prior restraint, or preventing the publication or discussion of ideas. This is in violation of the First Amendment of the U.S. Constitution. The authors examine several ways in which corporate media distorts the news, offering examples to illustrate these concepts. They conclude that independent media helps play an essential role in helping combat this distortion. Andy Lee Roth is associate director of Project Censored. Steve Macek is a professor of communication

"Corporate Media Harms Not Only Through Omission, But Also by Distortion," by Andy Lee Roth and Steve Macek, Truthout, November 15, 2021. Reprinted by permission.

Media Consolidation

and media studies at North Central College and co-coordinator of Project Censored's campus affiliate program.

As you read, consider the following questions:

1. What do the authors mean by "censorship" as it applies to Project Censored?
2. What is the harm caused by omitting important facts and perspectives from news coverage?
3. How can independent media help address the issues caused by corporate media, according to the authors?

From *The Washington Post's* investigation of the January 6 insurrection to *The Wall Street Journal's* series about Facebook and Reuters' examination of how "qualified immunity" protects police from prosecution for excessive force, establishment news outlets deserve credit for breaking a number of momentous stories in the past year. Yet, the establishment press missed, minimized, or mis-framed at least as many important stories as they covered thoroughly and accurately. That is why our organization, Project Censored, a nonprofit news watch, continues to monitor and identify the top 25 vital, sometimes earth-shaking stories that corporate news media ignore or distort each year.

Past critics have complained that the stories included in Project Censored's annual lists are not actually "censored" because some of them have been covered by "dozens of publications," albeit smaller, independent ones. Others point out that stories that appear on our list sometimes receive attention from "at least one major mainstream newspaper, magazine, [or] television news program." Such criticisms miss the point of Project Censored's work and gloss over significant gaps, biases and blockades in corporate media coverage that the Project exposes.

The "censored" stories that Project Censored lists in its annual story have not necessarily been completely and irrevocably

| 32

repressed by the government or some other powerful institution, such as big business or a political party.

Censorship in that specific sense is known in First Amendment law as "prior restraint," the direct effort to *prevent* publication or publicization of ideas or expression. That sort of censorship is relatively rare in the United States.

Instead, the independently reported stories that Project Censored highlights as "censored" have typically been subject to *partial* or *incomplete* corporate coverage. This indirect censorship is more subtle but no less consequential: The effects of underreporting or misreporting may ultimately be more harmful than nonreporting. Furthermore, an indirect blockade of news coverage need not be total in order for an issue to remain unknown to all but a small segment of the public that actively seeks reporting on that topic. Using stories drawn from Project Censored's 2020-2021 story list, we identify four recurring patterns of indirect censorship in corporate news coverage where the outlets failed to provide the coverage and context that these stories deserved based on their social significance and relevance to current political and cultural debates.

Important Facts and Perspectives Omitted

Consider, for instance, the historic wave of wildcat strikes for workers' rights since the onset of COVID-19, one story on the Project's 2020-2021 list. Responding to dangerous working conditions and stagnant wages, tens of thousands of U.S. service workers, drivers, health workers, teachers, and others have taken part in more than a thousand brief, impromptu, unauthorized work stoppages. This recent burst of labor unrest may go down in history as the largest wave of wildcat strikes since the early 1970s. Nevertheless, with the exception of isolated coverage in local and specialized corporate news outlets, for more than a year, until July 2021, establishment news outlets failed to cover these strikes in any depth, much less systematically.

Media Consolidation

THE FUTURE OF INDEPENDENT INVESTIGATIVE JOURNALISM

There has never been a greater need for independent, in-depth reporting, yet the news industry is largely failing to capitalize on that need. That failure is no secret: it is driving a decline in the public's appetite for newspapers and network television in numerous markets, and thus in revenues. It is also driving the emergence of new competitors for the public's attention. Wikileaks is one of those competitors; so are environmental groups like Greenpeace, which have effectively established their own news-gathering and distribution networks.

In the current situation, "stakeholder media"—outlets created and controlled by communities of practice or interest, with the goal of influencing organizations or their governance—will continue to grow in reach and power. This has implications for the content of investigative media, and also for their business models, and not least for their ethics.

Their content will be increasingly aimed at procuring an immediate and sustainable advantage for the communities that support them. That will certainly include practical information generated by media users as well as journalists—a function that was pioneered by internet-based user forums. Crowdsourcing will be expanded and refined. Stakeholder media will also feature more critical aggregation, sifting through masses of information to save their users time and search costs.

Their business models will depend less on exclusivity and more on sharing the benefits of networking than is currently the general case for independent media. On the one hand, exclusivity may not increase the social value of a given investigation; it also lessens a report's impact, because the fewer the number of people who know about a situation, the less likely it is to change. On the other, networking may enable independent media to form sufficiently large publics, through coalition, to generate attractive advertising bases, or markets for other serves (such as databases).

The ethics of investigative stakeholder media will shift (and are already shifting) from objectivity to transparency. There has always been a conflict in journalism between the neutral stance of objectivity

| 34

and the reformist drive of investigators; that conflict will become more acute. Transparency—the revelation of why journalists have sought and exposed certain information, and of how they did it, and in whose interests—will become more prominent.

The decline of the news industry—not only as an economic entity, but as a credible source of reliable information (another documented trend)—is an opportunity as well as a danger. Whether we like it or not—most journalists I know do not—it is well underway. So is the rise of stakeholder media. This is the new world, and the news world, that we have to live and work in from now on.

This is hardly novel in the history of journalism; so-called "objective" media became the mainstream of news media only within the past century, and only within certain regions. Media that defended the interests of specific communities or movements (or powers) were the rule, not the exception.

[...]

"Digital Media and the Future of Investigative Journalism," by Mark Lee Hunter, Open Society Foundations, May 30, 2011.

Without the context of an ongoing, national wave of wildcat strikes, reports of individual work stoppages here and there failed to convey the magnitude of locally organized worker resistance to pandemic working conditions. The only wildcat strike that attracted any sustained commercial media attention up until October 2021 (when reporting by corporate media on the current strike wave began belatedly to pick up) was the August 2020 National Basketball Association players' refusal to play in the aftermath of the police shooting of Black motorist Jacob Blake; work stoppages following the Blake shooting by WNBA and MLB teams also attracted some corporate media attention.

Discordant News Framed as "Opinion"

News that challenges the political and economic status quo is frequently framed as "opinion" or "commentary" by corporate news media. For example, independent outlets such as *The Nation*,

Media Consolidation

the *Guardian* and *The Intercept* have carefully chronicled the efforts of Canary Mission, a scandal-mongering website devoted to demonizing Israel's critics, and its impact on free speech rights. Dating back to 2019, establishment coverage of Canary Mission and the organization's McCarthyite tactics has been limited to an editorial in *The New York Times* by civil rights advocate Michelle Alexander. Similarly, reporting on how factory farming creates a perfect breeding ground for new diseases that can easily spread to humans was covered most thoroughly by small, independent investigative news outfits. Apart from a substantial report published by *Vox*, the only corporate coverage of note was an op-ed in the *Los Angeles Times*.

Isolated Corporate Coverage

Project Censored's 2020-2021 story list also includes several topics that were the subject of extensive and well-researched articles in a single major corporate newspaper or magazine but which never got picked up or investigated further by any other major news organization. For instance, Europe's hunger for biomass fuel made from American forests was the subject of an excellent *New York Times* article, but no other corporate news outlet so much as ran an op-ed on the topic. *The Atlantic* reprinted an article from *Hakai Magazine*, an online journal based in Canada that focuses on ecological issues, about the dire consequences of the darkening of coastal waters, another story on Project's 2020-2021 list, but no other corporate news outlet paid any attention to the topic whatsoever.

Blockaded Issues

Finally, some of the stories among this year's Top 25 have, in fact, been completely ignored by the corporate news media. The dangers and legal harassment facing journalists investigating global financial corruption, for instance, has received some attention from the corporate news media *outside* the United States, but virtually none at all domestically. YouTube's wholesale demonetizing of

| 36

progressive channels and video makers has been utterly overlooked by U.S. corporate media, even as they have run several stories about YouTube deplatforming right-wing pundits and politicians.

The Need for Independent Media

Corporate news media are guilty of both "sins of omission" (neglecting significant facts about important issues, failing to follow up on stories that challenge the status quo) and "sins of distortion" (framing news that contradicts conventional wisdom as "opinion," failing to interpret clearly interrelated events, such as the recent spate of wildcat strikes, as part of an overarching trend). This record of establishment press failure — amply documented by 45 years of Project Censored's annual story lists — underscores the vital necessity of independent news reporting. In counterpoint to the corporate media's narrow definitions of who and what count as newsworthy, which often reinforce deep-rooted inequalities, independent news outlets bring to light newsworthy stories that simultaneously expose social injustices and highlight compounding gaps and biases in corporate news coverage.

VIEWPOINT 4

> *"Media coverage can drive public perceptions of corporations and influence politicians' views. In particular, media coverage can amplify misdeeds of companies across states, which worries managers who do not want to see new regulations."*

Corporations Shape Politics, and the Media Often Can't Stop It

Richard A. Devine and Michael Holmes

In this viewpoint, Richard A. Devine and Michael Holmes examine the ways in which corporations shape politics. Broadly speaking, corporations use campaign donations to candidates supportive of them to exert this influence, but there are several situations in which corporations may view this as necessary. Corporations focus on state politics in states where they operate, since it will impact them if new regulations are created. They put a large amount of money into supporting candidates that are against regulation. One potential threat to their influence is negative news coverage of their company in a national media outlet, which prompts them to donate even more money to persuade candidates to continue to support them and voters to side with them. Richard A. Devine is an assistant professor of

"Money talks: Big business, political strategy and corporate involvement in US state politics," by Richard A. Devine and Michael Holmes, The Conversation, June 29, 2020. https://theconversation.com/money-talks-big-business-political-strategy-and-corporate-involvement-in-us-state-politics-140686. Licensed under CC BY-ND 4.0 International.

management at DePaul University. Michael Holmes is an associate professor of strategic management at Florida State University.

As you read, consider the following questions:

1. What types of industries did the authors study? Why did they choose these industries?
2. Do corporations spend more when local media reports on negative news related to a company?
3. What impacts can state regulations have on corporations?

P olitical spending by corporations is big business.
As one corporate executive with experience in business-government relations says, "A company that is dependent on government that does not donate to politicians is engaging in corporate malpractice."

Our research group heard that statement during a series of interviews with industry insiders that we conducted for a study on corporate political strategy and involvement in U.S state politics.

In the 2018 election cycle, for example, private interests spent US$500 million on campaign contributions to U.S. federal election candidates and nearly $7 billion to lobby federal officials.

As shown by campaign finance monitor the Center for Responsive Politics, those firms most affected by government regulation spend more. The operations of Facebook, for example, could be heavily affected by government legislation, whether from laws concerning net neutrality, data privacy, censorship or the company's classification as a platform or publisher. Facebook spent over $2 million in contributions and $24 million in lobbying during the same period.

This kind of political spending is also common across state governments. From Alaska to Alabama, firms spend huge sums of money to influence policymaking because they depend on their local business environments, resources and regulations.

For example, after *Citizens United*, a landmark 2010 U.S. Supreme Court decision that freed corporations (as well as nonprofits, unions and other associations) to spend unlimited amounts in elections, political spending skyrocketed. An examination of 16 states that provided pre-*Citizens United* data revealed that the 2018 election cycle saw over $540 million in independent spending across their state elections. This is compared with the 2007-2008 election cycle prior to the *Citizens United* ruling, in which independent spending in these states amounted to $106 million. That's an over five-fold increase.

As the next election approaches, corporate involvement in state politics is vital to understand. Companies' attempts to manage state regulations have important effects on their operations directly as well as on state revenues and on the lives of state residents. Corporations can affect the air that you breathe, the water that you drink and the taxes that you pay.

External Forces Spark Donations

A new study we conducted with colleagues Trey Sutton and Bruce Lamont provides insight into the details of when and why corporations contribute to state gubernatorial and legislative candidates.

We examined political contributions by publicly traded firms in elections for governor and the legislature across the 50 U.S. states. The companies we studied (e.g., ExxonMobil and 3M) all operate in environmentally intensive industries – oil and gas, chemical, energy and manufacturing industries. Specifically, the companies in these industries have industrial manufacturing processes that create toxic releases. We also interviewed industry insiders, political affairs consultants and lobbyists to complement our empirical findings.

At the core, firms spend when they are dependent on states, meaning that they have vested interests and operations in a state that are subject to regulation. Regulation creates uncertainty for managers – which they don't like. Spending helps alleviate the uncertainty by influencing what regulation may be imposed. Our study went beyond this observation, and had four major insights:

1. Companies Spend When They Are Worried About Negative Media Coverage Prompting What They Perceive to Be Potentially Harmful Regulations

As one executive told us, "We spend a lot of time tracking media and local advocacy groups. We track [them] on a daily basis, and I get a report each week."

Media coverage can drive public perceptions of corporations and influence politicians' views. In particular, media coverage can amplify misdeeds of companies across states, which worries managers who do not want to see new regulations. In line with this, we found that the firms spent 70% more in states they operated in when national media coverage of their companies was more negative rather than less negative.

We found that this effect was exclusive to national media coverage as opposed to local media coverage. Specifically, when local media coverage was more negative, it did not appear to affect political spending.

2. Firms Spend When There Are Powerful Social Movement Organizations—for Example, Environmental Protection Groups—Within a State

"Public relations firms are routinely engaged to monitor activists and the media, because if you don't watch them, they can create regulatory change. You have to get ahead of it," an executive said.

Social movement organizations (e.g., Sierra Club and the Rainforest Action Network) help shape public opinion on important issues, pursue institutional change and can prompt legal reform as well, which is a concern to corporations. Our research indicated that in states where they had operations, firms spent 102% more when facing greater opposition from social movement organizations than they would have on average.

3. Firms Spend to Gain a Seat at the 'Legislative Table' to Communicate Their Interests

A political affairs consultant and lobbyist said, "Regulations are a negotiation, there is not a logic, no rule of law, lobbyists come in here…" In essence, legislators rely on policy experts and analysts, among others, when crafting new legislation, but often, solutions can be unclear with competing demands and interests.

Our interviewees shared with us that companies spread their contributions around to those politicians who they believe will listen to their causes and concerns – regardless of party.

They described themselves as wanting their voices heard on particular issues and as important players in the states in which they operate due to the employment and tax base they bring to states.

Boeing, for example, is the largest private employer in the state of Washington and has been able to secure tax breaks as a result. This is despite documented environmental problems that Boeing's operations have had in the state.

4. Firms Spend Because They See It as Consistent with Their Responsibility to Stakeholders

"Companies mostly want certainty, they want to know the bottom line, and engagement can create opportunities," said one political affairs consultant.

Corporations have a legal and ethical responsibility to their stakeholders. Company leaders often believe they are upholding their responsibilities to shareholders, employees, communities, customers and suppliers by participating in the political process.

What Are the Stakes?

There can be huge repercussions for companies in state regulation. As one political affairs consultant told us, "[Regulation] is the pot at the end of the rainbow that could create endless possibilities of profit, it's the only thing that stands between them and unending profits…"

Ride hailing service Uber, for example, has mounted protracted political campaigns aimed at state legislatures and local governments to protect the company's interests. The result, among others: The ride hailing service has been able to get independent contractor status for their drivers in many states, which means the company does not have to provide unemployment insurance, workers' compensation and other benefits.

Passage of regulations in large states like California, for example, can have nearly as much impact as a national regulation – making their passage far more significant for companies working nationally.

For example, since California sets more stringent emissions standards for vehicles than most other states, manufacturers designing cars for the U.S. market must make sure their vehicles can pass these standards. In this way, California and other states following its lead pose a larger regulatory hurdle for auto manufacturers.

Where Does This Leave Us?

Taken together, corporate involvement in state politics is an important phenomenon. In addition to providing needed products and services, corporations bring jobs and increased investment to states, which can strengthen communities and state economies. Their operations also can bring health and environmental problems for state residents, however.

Given the changed business landscape – and increased operating costs – caused by the coronavirus pandemic, we expect that businesses across the country will continue to be interested in influencing policies ranging from workplace safety to local and state tax breaks. This interest will likely translate into significant spending in the upcoming election, to both major parties and their candidates.

And that political spending will affect everything from your wallet to your health.

VIEWPOINT

> "Misinformation is a fairly regular topic of conversation within the newsroom itself. About six-in-ten journalists (58%) say they had conversations with colleagues about misinformation at least several times a month over the past year."

News Organizations Need to Do More to Combat Misinformation

Jeffrey Gottfried, Amy Mitchell, Mark Jurkowitz, and Jacob Liedke

This viewpoint from the Pew Research Center considers how journalists view and attempt to address the issue of misinformation in news media. The majority of journalists are concerned, and many say they deal with false and made-up stories regularly. Unfortunately, there are few procedures in place at most media organizations to address false stories, and the need to quickly report on sensational stories in order to compete with other media organizations increases the risk. Jeffrey Gottfried is an associate director of research at Pew Research Center. Amy Mitchell was formerly the director of journalism research at Pew. Mark Jurkowitz is a senior writer at Pew Research Center and a former associate director of journalism research. Jacob Liedke is a research analyst at Pew.

"Journalists highly concerned about misinformation, future of press freedoms," by Jeffrey Gottfried, Amy Mitchell, Mark Jurkowitz, and Jacob Liedke, Pew Research Center, June 14, 2022.

As you read, consider the following questions:

1. What percent of journalists say they deal with false news on a fairly regular basis?
2. How do journalists feel about their ability to spot false news? How confident are they in their colleagues' ability to spot it?
3. What percent of journalists never cover issues of misinformation from politicians and public figures?

Amid efforts to fight false and made-up information, anti-media campaigns, increased lawsuits and global news crackdowns, journalists in the United States express great concern about the future of press freedoms.

Roughly six-in-ten journalists surveyed say they are either extremely (33%) or very concerned (24%) about potential restrictions on press freedoms in the U.S. About a quarter (23%) are somewhat concerned, while just one-in-five express low levels of concern about this.

Journalists See False and Made-Up News as a Big Problem and Don't Have Much Confidence in How the Industry Handles It

Another area of concern for journalists is the volume of erroneous information today. More than nine-in-ten journalists surveyed (94%) say made-up news and information is a significant problem in America today, with 71% identifying it as a very big problem and 23% seeing it as a moderately big problem; 6% say it is a small problem or not a problem at all.

The American public also sees made-up news and information as a problem, but not quite to the same extent. In a separate survey of 10,441 U.S. adults conducted March 7-13, 2022, 50% say made-up news is a very big problem (21 percentage points below journalists), while another 34% say it is a moderately big problem and 16% say it is a small problem or not a problem at all.

Media Consolidation

Misinformation is a fairly regular topic of conversation within the newsroom itself. About six-in-ten journalists (58%) say they had conversations with colleagues about misinformation at least several times a month over the past year.

The survey also finds that one-third of journalists indicate that they deal with false or made-up news in their work on a fairly regular basis – saying that they come across false information when working on a story either extremely often (8%) or fairly often (24%). Another 44% say they sometimes come across it.

About seven-in-ten journalists (71%) say they are either extremely (21%) or very confident (49%) in their ability to recognize false information when they are working on a story.

Still, specifically among reporting journalists, about a quarter (26%) say they unknowingly reported on a story that was later found to contain false information. (Reporting journalists are those who indicated in the survey that they report, edit or create original news stories *and* that they have one of the following job titles: reporter, columnist, writer, correspondent, photojournalist, video journalist, data visualization journalist, host, anchor, commentator or blogger. About three-quarters of all journalists in this study – 76% – are reporting journalists.)

While the journalists surveyed here may feel good about their own ability to detect misinformation, they are not particularly confident in the industry's ability to manage or correct it. Only 8% of all journalists surveyed say news organizations do a very good job at handling misinformation, while another 35% say news outlets are somewhat good at it – lower than the ratings journalists give news organizations on several other core functions.

And most say their news organization (or the main one they work for if they work for more than one) does *not* have formal guidance on how to handle made-up and false information in their jobs. Six-in-ten say their organization does not have guidelines for how to handle false and made-up information that they come across, far higher than the 36% who say their organization does.

Most Journalists Think It Is Important to Report on the False Statements of Public Figures

Most journalists think that part of managing misinformation means reporting on public figures who make false or made-up statements. Twice as many journalists say that if a public figure makes a statement that is false or made up, news organizations should "report on the statement because it is important for the public to know about" (64%) rather than "not report on the statement because it gives attention to the falsehoods and the public figure" (32%).

Many journalists, though, never or almost never cover the issue of misinformation. Two-thirds of journalists surveyed (66%) say almost none of the stories they worked on in the past year had to do with false or made-up information. Just 6% of those surveyed say half or more of the news stories they worked on covered false or made-up news in some way, while about a quarter (27%) say that some of their stories – but fewer than half – dealt with this topic.

Vast Majority of Journalists Are Against Requiring a License to Be a Journalist

One particular feature of journalism is that there is no requirement to have a license or certification process to call oneself a journalist – unlike a physician would in order to practice medicine in the United States. The question of whether to require one or not occasionally gets raised. As of now, a solid majority of journalists are against such a requirement. Nearly three-quarters of journalists (74%) are in favor of continuing to allow journalists to practice journalism without needing a license. One-quarter of U.S. journalists would like to see a license required for members of their industry.

Currently, there is no licensing requirement for journalists themselves. Radio and television stations are licensed and regulated by the Federal Communications Commission, but there is no such regulatory authority for newspapers and online outlets.

VIEWPOINT 6

> "The merger, of course, will also influence what information reaches Americans, including content citizens need to govern themselves in a democracy."

Media Consolidation Allows Corporations to Control the Information that Americans Can Access

Margot Susca

In this viewpoint, Margot Susca discusses the merger between Disney and 21st Century Fox, which were two of the largest film companies in the world at that time. When this viewpoint was originally published in 2017, the merger had not yet taken place (it would be completed in 2019), but Susca points out the danger of allowing major media companies to merge in this way. She points out that these mergers not only allow media companies to have excessive control over the cultural output Americans consume—which she argues already has an impact on democracy—but it also gives these corporations a great deal of influence over domestic and international governments. Margot Susca is an assistant professor of journalism at American University.

"Disney's potential 21st Century Fox merger continues troubling trend of media consolidation," by Margot Susca, The Conversation, December 21, 2017, https://theconversation.com/disneys-potential-21st-century-fox-merger-continues-troubling-trend-of-media-consolidation-89229. Licensed under CC BY-ND 4.0 International.

| 48

Does Media Consolidation Harm Democracy?

As your read, consider the following questions:

1. According to this viewpoint, what do studies indicate about how culture impacts Americans' attitudes?
2. How did Susca think Disney and 21st Century Fox would react to threats of regulation that could prevent the merger?
3. What impact does Susca believe the merger would have on a China-U.S. media alliance?

In the U.S., only a handful of media companies control what children and adults watch and read.

Now that number could get even smaller.

The proposed US$52.4 billion merger of Disney and 21st Century Fox would merge the first and third largest film companies in the world. Marvel Studios, Lucasfilm, Pixar, Searchlight, 20th Century Fox and Big Sky would all be under the same umbrella. Disney would also acquire control of TV channels like FX and National Geographic, adding to a portfolio that already includes ABC and ESPN. It would have majority stake in Hulu, which would position the streaming service to take on Netflix head-to-head in what many industry insiders expect will be a battle for market control.

As someone who studies global media power, I find the potential Disney-Fox merger troubling not just because one corporation will control production of narratives about popular culture and politics on television, film and streaming services, but because it will also create a media powerhouse worth so much that it could be as powerful as a state actor on the world stage.

Media Consolidation

'Weapons of Mass Distraction'

For children and adults, media isn't just entertainment. It is, in many ways, the tapestry of American life.

We grow up in front of the television screen, the silver screen and the computer screen, spending in the United States an astounding 12 hours daily engaged with media. It shapes our attitudes and beliefs, our likes and dislikes, our wants and desires and even our basic definitions of what it means to be normal.

Studies have found that Americans' attitudes about everything from terrorism to race relations are largely formed by what they watch and hear. For example, a 2015 study was able to show that negative stereotyping of Muslims in news reports led to increased support for military action against Muslim countries.

Meanwhile, fictional television shows like "Homeland," "The Americans" and "24" routinely cast foreigners as villains, making it easier for audiences to demonize citizens from other countries and immigrants. These attitudes have been shown to have a real effect on public policy.

Advertising to children is a $17 billion industry. According to the Campaign for a Commercial Free Childhood, children's ads have all been connected to "eating disorders, precocious sexuality, youth violence and family stress," while contributing to "children's diminished capability to play creatively."

As is the case with all businesses, the bottom line for media companies trumps any consideration of the public good. Studios ultimately produce shows that attract the most viewers and sell the most ads and movie tickets: cheaply produced reality television, celebrity gossip, political drama, and films packed with action and special effects.

The result is a media system that has become what media scholar Marty Kaplan calls a "weapon of mass distraction."

A Consolidation Frenzy

Media control, then, has powerful implications in our society: The stories that appear influence how citizens make sense of the world.

When journalist and media critic Ben Bagdikian wrote his 1983 book "The Media Monopoly," 50 companies controlled a majority of what Americans watched, read and heard.

Bagdikian predicted that further media consolidation of ownership would weaken coverage of lobbying, environmental issues, war, labor fights and corporate wrongdoing.

By the time he wrote his sequel in 2004, Bagdikian's predictions had largely come true. But even he didn't think that 90 percent of American media outlets would fall under the control of just five big media corporations. He wrote that these conglomerates operated as a kind of cartel that controlled our "most important institutions," from newspapers to film.

Disney, of course, was one of the five media conglomerates Bagdikian named. Another was Rupert Murdoch's News Corp., which, at the time, included parts of what would become 21st Century Fox.

Money Talks

If the $52 billion price tag sounds big, consider this: The payoff will be massive. The hybrid corporation control will give Disney a third of all domestic box office revenue, which, in 2017, amounted to about $3 billion.

Because the deal further shrinks the dwindling number of voices controlling media, Disney's merger with Fox has a long way to go to pass Department of Justice muster. Three major anti-trust laws are supposed to guide Department of Justice principles related to mergers and the resulting market conditions left in their wake.

Media Consolidation

But I expect we'll see what's happened in the past when regulators have attempted to control the ownership structure of other media conglomerates: a massive lobbying campaign. The $72 billion deal that merged Comcast and AT&T Broadband in 2001 was given the go-ahead. A decade later, Comcast bought NBC Universal for $30 billion, a merger that passed both FCC and Department of Justice scrutiny after being called a "lobbying frenzy" by Roll Call.

Disney already spends millions of dollars annually lobbying Congress, the U.S. State Department, the Federal Communications Commission and the Office of the U.S. Trade Representative, the federal agency responsible for negotiating with China to alter how it accepts and runs Hollywood films.

I also predict this merger will strengthen Disney's bargaining power with China, which controls film's release dates. China, the world's second-largest film market, typically blacks out American films during crucial summer blockbuster months to focus on domestic films, and it allows just 34 foreign films to be released each year. Yet some believe China will be more willing to negotiate with the mega-company that will emerge after the merger because of its sheer financial clout.

The merger, of course, will also influence what information reaches Americans, including content citizens need to govern themselves in a democracy.

Disney shares members of its board of directors with companies like Anheuser-Busch, Chase Manhattan, Coca-Cola, Unilever and Pfizer. Citizens should ask: How might this influence the information disseminated about food, banking regulations, consumer products and pharmaceuticals?

And consider how a stronger China-U.S. media alliance could impact U.S. films, television and news. Would American media companies be hesitant to cover human

Does Media Consolidation Harm Democracy?

rights violations, factory conditions or pollution in Asia for fear that they would anger the Chinese government and, therefore, lose bargaining power and access to audiences?

What gets left out of coverage is sometimes as important as what makes it in.

If just four companies get to decide, we should all be concerned.

Media Consolidation

Periodical and Internet Sources Bibliography

The following articles have been selected to supplement the diverse views presented in this chapter.

McKay Coppins, "A Secretive Hedge Fund Is Gutting Newsrooms," the *Atlantic,* October 14, 2021. https://www.theatlantic.com/magazine/archive/2021/11/alden-global-capital-killing-americas-newspapers/620171/.

Alex Cosh, "The Corporate Takeover of Canadian News Media Is Accelerating," *Jacobin*, July 7, 2023. https://jacobin.com/2023/07/canada-news-media-toronto-star-postmedia-nordstar-journalism-corporate-takeover.

Elizabeth Djinis, "Can Local News Be Saved?" Poynter, August 2, 2022. https://www.poynter.org/reporting-editing/2022/can-local-news-be-saved/.

Rod Dreher, "I Don't Believe the Media," *American Conservative*, June 12, 2020. https://www.theamericanconservative.com/i-dont-believe-the-media/.

Willa Frank, "Media Consolidation Is Threatening the Spirit of Journalism," the *Register Forum*, March 23, 2020. https://registerforum.org/11359/opinion/media-consolidation-is-threatening-the-spirit-of-journalism/.

Nick Licata, "How We Got Here: The Toxicity of Media Consolidation on Our Democracy," Post Alley Seattle, March 29, 2021. https://www.postalley.org/2021/03/29/how-we-got-here-the-toxicity-of-media-consolidation-on-our-democracy/.

John Nichols, "Local News Has Been Destroyed. Here's How We Can Revive It," the *Nation*, December 25, 2023/January 1, 2024. https://www.thenation.com/article/society/local-news-revival-plan/.

Hamilton Nolan, "Public Funding of Journalism Is the Only Way," How Things Work, February 5, 2024. https://www.hamiltonnolan.com/p/public-funding-of-journalism-is-the.

Thomas Schatz, "How 2 Companies Came to Dominate the Media Business," the *Nation*, December 25, 2023/January 1, 2024. https://www.thenation.com/article/society/netflix-disney-media-consolidation.

Christian Schneider, "The Link Tax: Government-Subsidized State Media," the *National Review*, November 9, 2023.https://www.nationalreview.com/2023/11/the-link-tax-government-subsidized-state-media/.

Matthew Sheffield, "Local News Isn't Dying Out: It's Being Killed Off by Corporate Greed," *Salon*, March 23, 2018. https://www.salon.com/2018/03/23/local-news-isnt-dying-out-its-being-killed-off-by-corporate-greed.

Alex Shephard, "Make Media Small Again: Why Consolidation Is Bad for Journalism—and How the Government Can Fix It," the *New Republic*, December 22, 2020. https://newrepublic.com/article/160562/media-consolidation-bad-journalism-democracy.

CHAPTER 2

Does Media Consolidation Negatively Impact Culture?

Chapter Preface

As the last chapter demonstrated, media consolidation and corporate influence have a powerful effect on news organizations, and that can also have a powerful effect democracy. The authors in this chapter take a look at what happens to culture when media is consolidated under the control of a few large corporations. For the purposes of this chapter, culture refers to the arts, and the viewpoints in this chapter focus specifically on books, movies, television, and music.

Mergers and acquisitions in the film and television industry have caused old brands and favorite channels to change or even disappear. One of the viewpoints here takes a close look at why that happens and why profit-seeking corporations often make decisions that disappoint many of their viewers. As far as the health of the media goes, the viewoint argues this can be both a bad development and a potentially good one.

Another author in this chapter examines how small and medium-sized book publishers are ill-equipped to step into the world of digital publishing. This, he argues, leaves them at a serious disadvantage with their larger, more tech-savvy competitors.

The last two viewpoints explore the impact of the internet and streaming on culture and mass communication. While in the 20th century media consolidation caused people to consume a relatively homogenous selection of media, the rise of the internet, streaming, and social media platforms has allowed for greater cultural output and distribution, allowing people to find culture and communities that really resonate with them.

VIEWPOINT 1

> "Big media companies are merging
> with or buying other big media
> companies. Some of the companies
> that were bought may soon be
> sold. Just about every company in
> Hollywood has been cutting costs and
> laying off employees."

Mergers and Consolidations Are Reshaping TV and Film Industries

Terry Gross

In this excerpted viewpoint Terry Gross interviews media and entertainment journalist Lucas Shaw about the many changes affecting the television and film industries in today's corporate environment. The distinct identities and brands of independent channels and media companies become lost as they're absorbed into larger media companies, changing the experience of consuming media. Shaw considers the collapse of cable television to be largely responsible for this shift in television and film media. The following interview took place during the 2023 writers' and actors' strikes, when the future of the industry felt particularly uncertain. Terry Gross is an American journalist and producer/host of NPR's interview-based radio program Fresh Air.

©2023 National Public Radio, Inc. NPR news report titled "Is the TV/Film Industry Collapsing, or Just Reshaping Itself for the Future?" by Terry Gross was originally published on npr.org on July 21, 2023, and is used with the permission of NPR. Any unauthorized duplication is strictly prohibited.

| 58

Does Media Consolidation Negatively Impact Culture?

As you read, consider the following questions:

1. What reasons does Gross give in this viewpoint for the upheaval in the entertainment industry?
2. What is Shaw's response to Gross's question about why all these mergers are happening? What does streaming have to do with it?
3. What advantages to the new media landscape does Shaw mention?

The entertainment industry is in upheaval. Writers and actors are on strike, and streamers are reckoning with not being profitable. Bloomberg reporter Lucas Shaw talks about what viewers can expect.

TERRY GROSS, HOST: This is FRESH AIR. I'm Terry Gross. The movie and TV industries are in chaos. Striking actors and writers have shut down production. Broadcast TV lost viewers to cable. Then cable lost viewers to streaming TV. Now broadcast cable and many streaming platforms are in trouble. The movie industry is in trouble, too. People spend more time and money on video games than on movies and more time watching YouTube than any other TV network. Big media companies are merging with or buying other big media companies. Some of the companies that were bought may soon be sold. Just about every company in Hollywood has been cutting costs and laying off employees. Is the industry collapsing or just reshaping? And what does this mean for viewers and for the future of entertainment?

My guest, Lucas Shaw, is the managing editor for media and entertainment at Bloomberg and the author of the weekly newsletter Screentime. He spent more than a decade writing about how the world's largest technology companies have reshaped pop culture.

Lucas Shaw, welcome to FRESH AIR. I think one way to show how movies and TV are changing is to look at who owns what. Which megacompanies are the biggest players, and what do they

59 |

Media Consolidation

own? So can we do some, like, media genealogy? So why don't we start with Warner Bros. Discovery?

LUCAS SHAW: So Warner Bros. Discovery is the combination of three companies that used to be independent. There was Discovery Communications, which is best known for a bunch of cable networks, including its namesake — you know, generally lowbrow reality TV. There was Scripps Networks, which was another kind of bundle of cable networks that included HGTV, the Food Network. And then there's Time Warner, which is sort of the big one of them all, which is home to the Warner Bros. film and television studio, cable networks like TNT and TBS as well as HBO. And Time Warner has been through a lot of mergers over the years. You know, it was famously combined with AOL, then separated and then was acquired by AT&T, the phone company, turned into a division called WarnerMedia, then spun out of that and merged with Discovery into Warner Bros. Discovery.

GROSS: My head is spinning.

SHAW: I think the employees at those companies feel the same way.

GROSS: Let me just say here, we think of all these, you know, channels and companies that you mentioned as being these independent companies with their own identities. And now all the ones you just mentioned are merged into this one giant company. So do brands stop meaning anything?

SHAW: Well, we're in the middle of a great reshuffling of what brands mean, right? So for the past several decades, people watched TV by watching broadcast networks and cable networks. And those were brands that rose and mattered quite a bit. You know, in my childhood, that was Nickelodeon and MTV and ESPN and all these cable networks that became among the most sort of beloved brands for young people and people of all ages. And streaming and the rise of internet media has changed all that because the cable networks have started to decline, and so a lot of them are being sold off, being combined, being rebranded.

GROSS: So let's continue our genealogy and move to Disney.

SHAW: So Disney in the last 20 years or so bought Pixar, the animation studio. It bought Marvel, the comic book factory. It bought Lucasfilm, which is the company that made and owned all the "Star Wars" movies. And then a few years ago, it bought many entertainment assets from Rupert Murdoch from his Fox company, which included some major television studios, TV networks like FX as well as the movie studio.

GROSS: And Paramount Global — what do they own?

SHAW: Paramount Global owns everything from the CBS broadcast network to cable networks — MTV, Comedy Central, VH1. It's in the process of trying to sell BET, which it owns. And it's the combination of two companies — CBS and Viacom — which have been sort of put together and split apart over the years but are currently all one under the Redstone family, this time Shari Redstone, who's the daughter of legendary media mogul Sumner Redstone.

GROSS: So why is this happening now? Is this happening to please shareholders? Is this happening because companies just want the edge in the competition and they want as little competition as possible? What's this about?

SHAW: It largely stems from the slow collapse of cable television. So most of the biggest media and entertainment companies of sort of the prior generation — many of them today make a lot of their money, if not most of their money, from cable networks. So Paramount, which we talked about, makes most of its money from

Media Consolidation

a bunch of cable networks. Disney doesn't make the majority, but it makes a lot of its money from cable networks. But the number of people who pay for cable or pay for satellite or other forms of television have been in decline for several years now, and the pace of that decline has picked up. Now, these cable networks make money from a couple of, in a couple of ways. They make money from the fees that they get from distributors like Comcast and Charter, and then they make money from advertising. The advertising market, after many, many years of increasing, has basically stopped growing. It's declined for some, but all the growth in advertising is in online media.

The money that they get from distributors is very affected because if you went from having 95 million people paying for your channel to now 80 or 75, that just — even if you get increases in the rate, you're just not going to make as much money from that. And so all these media companies saw sort of the writing on the wall for the business of cable TV. They're trying to manage that decline 'cause they still generate a lot of profit from it. But they have responded by both creating their own streaming services, which they see as sort of the future, mostly because of the success that Netflix has had, or then merging because they see opportunities to cut costs by combining people. They get more power in the marketplace. If you are negotiating with a Comcast and you own 20 cable networks instead of 10 cable networks, Comcast has a harder time pushing you around.

GROSS: If one company owns all these different channels and some of them are niche channels like Turner Classic Movies or HBO, how much does the parent company really care about the identity of individual channels? — 'cause it all just becomes about making profit and, you know, beating out the competition. So some things that are really valuable can't just be measured in profit and in measuring yourself against the metrics of other companies. So am I wrong to be worried about individual identities being slowly eradicated?

SHAW: I think it depends on which individual identities matter to you. So you're correct that a lot of these networks, brands that have been built up over the years that people may have some attachment to are going away or at least being starved, right? You know, a lot of these media companies have shifted resources from cable networks to streaming or are focusing resources on a few networks. So in the case of Warner Bros. Discovery, there was a moment in time where they were making original programming for TNT and TBS and some of those networks. They're not really doing that anymore. Or you — we've talked about Turner Classic Movies. That's a brand that they feel they've invested too much money in, and so they are cutting back the investment in a significant way.

You know, Disney has spoken recently. Bob Iger, the CEO, gave an interview in which he called his TV assets non-core, which was his way of saying they're for sale. And that means that a network that's been around for decades like ABC is potentially in play. And so if you — if that really matters to you, certainly for the employees at those companies, for some of the viewers, that's frightening. The counterargument to that is that new brands have been created, and so maybe if you really like Hulu or if you really like Disney+, that's sort of the replacement for what ABC has been for many decades.

[…]

VIEWPOINT

> "Despite the numerous benefits that books have to offer, the publishing industry that powers their production, continues to face a plethora of unprecedented challenges."

Small and Medium Publishers Aren't Ready for the New Business Model

Mike Harman

Corporate mergers are affecting not only newspapers, television, and film. They're also having a huge impact on the book publishing industry. In this viewpoint, Mike Harman explores several reasons small and medium-sized publishers are at a disadvantage in today's increasingly consolidated publishing environment. These disadvantages primarily involve the rising costs of production and operation and a lack of market information, challenges that their larger competitors often don't struggle with as much. The rise of digital publishing has also added an element of uncertainty to the publishing industry. Mike Harman is senior vice president of business development at Hurix Digital.

"6 Common Challenges Faced By Small and Medium Publishers," by Mike Harman, KITABOO, March 13, 2023. Reprinted by permission.

As you read, consider the following questions:

1. What are some of the challenges small and medium-sized publishers face, according to Harman?
2. What impact has the digital era had on book publishing?
3. In this viewpoint, the author says that small and medium-sized publishers often lack the technical skill and expertise to compete in today's publishing world. Why is that?

In an era where continuous information bombardment has become the order of the day, books serve as a tiny oasis of knowledge, enigma, and depth. Not only do they work wonders in reducing stress, enhancing knowledge, and improving vocabulary, but they also provide an excellent opportunity for mental stimulation and cognitive engagement.

However, despite the numerous benefits that books have to offer, the publishing industry that powers their production, continues to face a plethora of unprecedented challenges. Small and medium publishers have to consistently grapple with issues like inadequate financial access, high transaction costs, low R&D expenditure, and lack of market information. Consequently, the growth and development of the Indian publishing industry have remained stagnated at around $2 billion since 2012.

As a small publisher, therefore, if you want to expand your network and enhance your revenues, you would first need to identify and delineate the specific challenges that your publishing house faces. It is only then that you would be able to formulate a well-equipped redressal strategy.

Media Consolidation

Top 6 Common Challenges Faced by Small and Medium Sized Digital Publishers

1. Changing Demands

With changing times, the demands of readers as well as authors are undergoing a significant transformation. While readers are becoming more focused, organized, and tech-savvy, authors are looking to create interactive, customized content. Small publishers, however, are not able to keep pace with these ever-changing demands. In order to cater to them, publishers will have to work towards improving their functionalities, developing interactive applications, and creating multimedia content.

2. Inconsistent Revenues

The financial models of small and medium publishers that used to work quite efficiently before are simply not relevant anymore. The benefits of financial access are now being largely accrued by large enterprises whereas small publishers are left to fend for themselves. This inconsistency has dealt a fatal blow to the modern publishing business. For correcting this scenario, publishers will have to diversify their channels of financing, smoothen their accounting processes and conduct a detailed credit risk analysis. Doing so will enable them to streamline their costs.

3. Digital Disruption

The emergence of the digital era has unleashed a variety of new possibilities – especially in the publishing sector. More and more readers are now shifting to the online space. Small and medium publishers, nevertheless, have not been able to match up to this digital disruption. Instead, they have become its unintended victims! If SMEs aim to survive and adapt to the future, they will need to transform the way they create, channelize, and distribute content. The opportunities that arrive with digital infrastructure will have to be availed so that the entire publishing business can be reoriented to suit the contemporary needs, demands, and requirements.

Judge Sides with Publishers in Internet Archive Suit

A federal judge has ruled in favor of a group of book publishers who sued the nonprofit Internet Archive in the early days of the coronavirus pandemic for scanning and lending digital copies of copyrighted books.

The four publishing houses — Hachette Book Group, HarperCollins, John Wiley & Sons and Penguin Random House — accused the Internet Archive of "mass copyright infringement" for loaning out digital copies of books without compensation or permission from the publishers.

Though libraries typically license e-books from publishers, the Internet Archive said it practiced "controlled digital lending," which argues that entities that own physical copies of books can lend out scanned versions.

The Internet Archive, which strives to provide "universal access to all knowledge," said its online library is legal under the doctrine of fair use.

But on Friday, U.S. District Court Judge John G. Koeltl of the Southern District of New York sided with the publishers, saying established law was on their side.

"At bottom, IA's fair use defense rests on the notion that lawfully acquiring a copyrighted print book entitles the recipient to make an unauthorized copy and distribute it in place of the print book, so long as it does not simultaneously lend the print book," Koeltl said in his opinion.

"But no case or legal principle supports that notion. Every authority points the other direction."

Koeltl noted that the Internet Archive can still scan and publish copies of books that are in the public domain.

The Authors Guild, a professional organization for published writers, praised the ruling, saying that "scanning & lending books w/out permission or compensation is NOT fair use—it is theft & it devalues authors' works." The Association of American Publishers said the ruling reaffirmed the importance of copyright law.

The Internet Archive said it will appeal the ruling.

"A judge sided with publishers in a lawsuit over the Internet Archive's online library," by Joe Hernandez, National Public Radio Inc. (NPR), March 26, 2023.

Media Consolidation

4. Lack of Know-How

The publishing industry, as it exists today, suffers a major 'know-how' crisis. Be it in terms of technology, networks, staff, market, information, or access – the lack of proper knowledge, skill, and expertise is literally glaring. To top it, small publishers have very little experience of dealing with domestic or international markets that exist outside their domain. The only credible way to resolve this problem is for SMEs to invest in developing in-house capabilities. In the absence of these, such publishers will only end up flailing through the choppy waters of modern publishing.

5. Royalty Management

For small and medium publishers, appropriate royalty management has also turned out to be a major challenge. The legal documents that define the complex partnership between copyright owners and publishers need to be well-defined. Furthermore, the relationship between intellectual property rights holders and supply chain partners too has to be classified in a diligent and adroit way. Most SMEs do not focus on this aspect, thus rendering their businesses vulnerable to legal challenges. By making sure that royalties are managed in time and all legal facets are clearly delineated in the contract, any such issue can easily be avoided.

6. Increased Competition

Last but not the least, many small publishers, as they function today, have to bear the brunt of increased market competition. Such competition primarily exists because economic integration and globalization have collectively caused many multinational companies to enter new markets. As a result, SMEs in the publishing sector are left to endure many cut-throat rivalries. While this appears to be a tough situation to get out of, the truth is – it is not! Publishers, across the board, just need to make one small change in their operations – they need to specialize! By developing specialized niches in their publications, small and medium publishers would be able to fulfill consumer demands and still stand up to the competition.

To Sum Up

As the world of manual publishing steadily begins to take a step back while being replaced by digital technology, small and medium publishers, across the world, will continue to face a multitude of challenges. Be it inefficient revenue models, limited sponsorship options, unsuitable delivery channels, or restricted staffing requirements – publishers who'll prefer to stick to their age-old guns, will certainly not be able to keep up.

In such a difficult scenario, the only way for the publishing industry in general and small publishers in particular, to survive, would be by identifying their specific challenges and rectifying them with the assistance of modern tools and techniques. Doing so would enable them to adapt well, perform better, and thus, keep their businesses thriving.

So, what are you waiting for? Get down to addressing every common challenge coming your way and gain a decisive edge over your competitors now!

VIEWPOINT 3

> *"Too many executives in too many industries, such as entertainment, tech and journalism, recognize generative AI for what it is: an opportunity to wield leverage over already precarious workforces."*

The Drive for Profit Is Causing Companies to Use AI to Replace Human Creators, but the Humans Are Fighting Back

Brian Merchant

A previous viewpoint in this chapter referred to the writers' strike. Hollywood writers had several complaints with their corporate bosses, and this viewpoint by Brian Merchant focuses on one of those issues: the use of artificial intelligence to write screenplays. However, as the author points out, the problem is not just for Hollywood writers. AI offers corporations the opportunity to generate content at a lower cost by employing fewer human writers. However, many people consider this unethical, and some speculate that it may be a ploy to undermine writers so they'll accept lower pay and less desirable conditions for working. However, some corporations have taken a stand against this and adopted "human first" policies to prevent AI-generated content from being published. Brian Merchant is an author and at the time this viewpoint was published was a tech columnist for the Los Angeles Times.

"Column: Your boss wants AI to replace you. The writers' strike shows how to fight back," by Brian Merchant, *Los Angeles Times*, May 11, 2023. Reprinted by permission.

As you read, consider the following questions:

1. What is the motive, according to Merchant, of making the rise of AI seem inevitable?
2. How do production companies plan to use AI to replace scriptwriters, according to sources cited in this viewpoint?
3. What industries beyond film and television are being damaged by the trend toward using AI for writing and illustration?

So far, the story of the AI boom has been the one that the tech industry has wanted to tell: Silicon Valley companies creating AI services that can mimic human art and words and, according to them, replace millions of jobs and transform the economy.

The next chapter is about humans fighting back. If the robots are rising, then a rebellion is taking shape to stop them — and its vanguard can be seen in the crowds of striking writers assembled across Hollywood.

One of those workers put it to me bluntly on the picket line, where screenwriters were protesting, among other things, the entertainment industry's openness to using artificial intelligence to churn out scripts: "F— ChatGPT."

But it's not just screenwriters — the movement includes illustrators, freelance writers and digital content creators of every stripe. "Every day," the artist and activist Molly Crabapple tells me, "another place that used to hire human artists has filled the spot with schlock from [AI image generator] Midjourney. If illustrators want to remain illustrators in two years, they have to fight now."

Each week brings more companies announcing they will replace jobs with AI, Twitter threads about departments that have been laid off, and pseudo-academic reports about how vulnerable millions of livelihoods are to AI. So, from labor organizing to class-action lawsuits to campaigns to assert the immorality of using AI-generated works, there's an increasingly aggressive effort taking shape to protect jobs from being subsumed or degraded by AI.

Media Consolidation

Their core strategies include refusing to submit to the idea that AI content generation is "the future," mobilizing union power against AI exploitation, targeting copyright violations with lawsuits and pushing for industrywide bans against the use of cheap AI material.

They're just getting started. And for the sake of everyone who is not a corporate executive, a middle manager or an AI startup founder, we'd better hope it works.

A big reason that the AI hype machine has been in overdrive, issuing apocalyptic claims about its vast power, is that the companies selling the tools want to make it all feel inevitable — to *feel* like the future — and have you believe that resisting it is both futile and stupid. Conveniently, most of these discussions eschew questions such as: *Whose* future? Whose future does AI really serve?

The answer to that is "Big Tech" and, to a lesser degree, "your boss."

The AI Now Institute, a consortium of AI researchers and policy experts, recently published a report that concluded the AI industry is "foundationally reliant on resources that are owned and controlled by only a handful of big tech firms." Its power is extremely concentrated in Silicon Valley, among giants such as Google and Meta, and that is where the economic benefits are all but certain to accrue.

OpenAI, which has a $10-billion partnership with Microsoft, is in particular making the case that its tools can replace workers — a study the company conducted with the University of Pennsylvania claimed its AI services could affect 80% of American workers; for 1 in 5, it could do half the tasks that constitute their jobs. OpenAI is marketing its services to consulting firms, ad agencies and studio executives, among many others.

Fortunately, as the AI Now report points out, "there is nothing about artificial intelligence that is inevitable."

The writers' strike, in particular, has brought to the forefront questions about how AI will replace or degrade human work, and it's given workers in other industries that stand to be affected a model response: Draw a line in the sand. Say no to cheap AI that lets executives drive down wages and erode your working conditions. Push back.

In its latest contract proposal, the Writers Guild of America asked that the entertainment industry agree not to use AI to replace writers. The industry declined, agreeing only to "annual meetings to discuss advancements in technology," throwing red flags up all over the place. It's one of the issues the studios refused to budge on, along with more routine demands such as pay increases, so the writers have brought the nation's entertainment industry to a halt. They do so in order to protect the very future of their trade.

I went down to the picket line at 20th Century Studios, where dozens of writers spent the day walking back and forth along Pico Boulevard. I wanted to ask the writers how they felt about AI, so I put the question to the first writer willing to talk.

That was when I heard the profane response quoted above. It came from Matt Nicholas, a 30-year-old writer and WGA member, who was all too aware exactly how AI was going to be used by the film and television industry — not to *replace* writers, but to undermine them.

"I have heard executives say that this is going to be the future," Nicholas said. That future being that the studios will use AI text generators to produce a script, however shoddy, and then "hire us to do rewrites of that material, which they're going to treat as source material."

Studios pay lower rates for script rewrites, and many writers worry it would actually be *more* work for them to correct and improve the boilerplate output, so it's simply a way for the industry to slash pay and break worker power. "It's absolutely ridiculous."

"It feels like the shoe that's about to drop," said another writer, Nastassja Kayln, "and they're hanging it over our heads on a regular basis."

"The same thing's going to happen to other industries," she added, "not just ours."

Media Consolidation

Indeed. It's already happening to other industries, and ones where workers have far less organized power or protections. As such, illustrators and artists have been the most aggressive in standing up to the AI companies — which makes sense, given that their battle is perhaps more existential.

A trio of illustrators has launched a class-action lawsuit alleging that the AI image generators Midjourney and Stable Diffusion trained their language models on copyrighted material, and now produce derivative works without the owners' consent. Meanwhile, the Center for Artistic Inquiry and Reporting has published an open letter written by Crabapple and journalist Marisa Mazria Katz, the center's executive director, calling on editorial outlets and newsrooms to "restrict AI illustration from publishing" altogether.

"This is an economic choice for society," the letter reads. "While illustrators' careers are set to be decimated by generative-AI art, the companies developing the technology are making fortunes. Silicon Valley is betting against the wages of living, breathing artists through its investment in AI." At the time of writing, it had more than 2,700 signatories, including MSNBC host Chris Hayes, author Naomi Klein, actor John Cusack and Laszlo Jakab Orsos, vice president of arts and culture at the Brooklyn Public Library.

"I saw my work in the LAION-5B dataset used to train Stable Diffusion," Crabapple says. "I saw DALL-E's ability to churn out bastard versions of my work with the prompt 'drawn by Molly Crabapple.' I saw how tech corporations, backed by billions of dollars, had gobbled up my work and the work of countless other artists to train products whose goal is to replace us."

AI generators, she notes, are cheaper and faster than humans, and most corporations won't care too much about quality — they'll happily use the synthesized works to replace artists, while the tech giants profit. "It's the biggest art heist in history."

A lot of outlets already would hesitate to publish AI-generated art for fear of blowback — the petition, built on the personal experience of many artists who've seen their work exploited, aims to formalize such instincts into policy.

| 74

"There is no ethical way to use the major AI image generators," Crabapple says. "All of them are trained on stolen images, and all of them are built for the purpose of deskilling, disempowering and replacing real, human artists. They have zero place in any newsroom or editorial operation, and they should be shunned."

While Crabapple and CAIR are focused primarily on artists' rights, editorial workers in journalism, magazines and beyond are also starting to formulate human-first responses to AI.

Staff at magazines, including small science fiction publications such as Clarkesworld and industry leaders such as Wired, have made it clear that they will not accept AI-generated submissions. Freelance writers and digital content creators, meanwhile, are in the trenches, giving testimony at the U.S. Copyright Office and organizing a defense against the companies and outlets that appear to be seeking to automate content production.

And the Freelance Solidarity Project, a part of the National Writers Union, has begun discussions about how best to organize around the subject. The worry is that the most precarious writers, artists and digital content creators are at risk of being swept away by AI and that their work, already barely protected, is being unfairly consumed by the maw of the for-profit large language models.

"Any creative work that exists online is currently 'fair game' to be scraped to train AI engines and build economic value for those companies without regard for either the copyright or consent of the original creators," Alexis Gunderson, a member of the Freelance Solidarity Project, tells me. "For many independent writers and artists, this reasonably feels like theft; for others, it can feel like an artistic violation."

Worse, "there is also the very real fear — which the WGA strike is so successfully highlighting — that much of the work that digital media workers currently do, both as freelancers and in staff roles, is likely to be first on the chopping block once these LLMs get robust enough," Gunderson says. "Which, in too many cases, they already are."

Media Consolidation

Freelancers, who don't have the benefit of union power to protect them from AI, are exploring other options, such as asserting moral rights to their work, and pressing the U.S. Copyright Office to make it easier to register — and protect — their published articles. But anxieties remain high, especially for less established and more vulnerable writers.

Finally, the online voices ringing out against AI have been surprisingly vigorous. Huge communities on Twitter, Reddit and other social media networks have called out the shoddiness and exploitative bent of the AI generation industry, and all this protest is already having an impact — beyond the strike, beyond the editorial policies and right down to the vibes, you could say. The sharing of AI-generated images online, for one thing, has gone from seeming cool and even a little spooky to lamer than an account with a blue check mark.

But there's a long way to go. Too many executives in too many industries, such as entertainment, tech and journalism, recognize generative AI for what it is: an opportunity to wield leverage over already precarious workforces. There's going to be a long, hard struggle, but it's one worth fighting. The result will determine what kind of work we all get to do; who technology ultimately serves, us or the 1%; and whether we all profit from the rise of AI — or just those who own the algorithms.

VIEWPOINT 4

> "More than any other, the field of mass communication transmits culture. At the same time, it helps institutional society try to understand itself and whether its structures are working."

How Mass Media Impacts Culture

Mark Poepsel

In this excerpted viewpoint, Mark Poepsel examines what mass media is and how it impacts culture, along with how it's changed over time. Mass media allows cultural knowledge to spread and creates a common experience between people that helps shape society, and the internet has had a significant impact on mass media. While in the past people largely consumed news from the same sources and watched many of the same TV shows and movies, the internet has allowed more cultural creators to put out their work and cultural consumers to find content that aligns with their interests. This has caused a decline in a lot of mass media, but it hasn't spelled the end of mass communication. Instead, social media platforms like X, Facebook, and YouTube are now where most mass communication is located. This has resulted in a process called convergence, where all media comes together through the internet and people can choose what media resonates the most with them. In this sense, the internet has taken some of the power over deciding which cultural works reach mass audiences away from media conglomerates. Mark Poepsel is

"Media, Society, Culture, and You," by Mark Poepsel, Rebus Press, 2018, https://press. rebus.community/mscy/chapter/chapter-1/. Licensed under CC BY 4.0 International.

Media Consolidation

an associate professor of mass communication at Southern Illinois University Edwardsville.

As you read, consider the following questions:

1. According to this viewpoint, what is society? What is culture?
2. What does Poepsel predict about the future of mass communication channels?
3. What are the three main types of cultural works Poepsel mentions? What are the differences between them?

It has been noted that a society is made up of small groups, larger communities, and vast institutions. A more complete definition of the term comes from the field of sociology. A society is a very large group of people organized into institutions held together over time through formalized relationships. Nations, for example, are made up of formal institutions organized by law. Governments of different size, economic institutions, educational institutions and others all come together to form a society.

By comparison, culture — the knowledge, beliefs, and practices of groups large and small — is not necessarily formalized. Culture is necessary for enjoying and making sense of the human experience, but there are few formalized rules governing culture.

Mass communication influences both society and culture. Different societies have different media systems, and the way they are set up by law influences how the society works. Different forms of communication, including messages in the mass media, give shape and structure to society. Additionally, mass media outlets can spread cultural knowledge and artistic works around the globe. People exercise cultural preferences when it comes to consuming media, but mass media corporations often decide which stories to tell and which to promote, particularly when it comes to forms of mass media that are costly to produce such as major motion pictures, major video game releases and global news products.

More than any other, the field of mass communication transmits culture. At the same time, it helps institutional society try to understand itself and whether its structures are working.

The Mass Media Dynamic

The mass media system is an institution itself. What sets it apart is its potential to influence the thinking of massive numbers of individuals. In fact, the ideas exchanged in organizational communication and interpersonal communication are often established, reinforced or negated by messages in the mass media. This is what it means for societies "to exist in transmission, in communication." Different types of communication influence each other.

But the mass media are also shaped and influenced by social groups and institutions. This is the nature of the mass media dynamic.

Individuals and groups in society influence what mass media organizations produce through their creativity on the input side and their consumption habits on the output side. It is not accurate to say that society exists within the mass media or under mass media "control." Social structures are too powerful for mass media to completely govern how they operate. But neither is it accurate to say that the mass media are contained within societies. Many mass media products transcend social structures to influence multiple societies, and even in societies that heavily censor their mass media the news of scandals and corruption can get out. The mass media and society are bound together and shape each other.

Almost everything you read, see and hear is framed within a mass media context; however, mere familiarity is no guarantee of success. Products in the mass media that fail to resonate with audiences do not last long, even if they seem in tune with current tastes and trends.

[…]

Mass Media Growth and Consolidation

As mass production of all sorts of manufactured goods grew during the 20th century, so did advertising budgets and the concept of brands. Brand advertising became fuel for the mass media, and as profitability rose, newspapers were bought up and organized into chains throughout the 20th century. Many newspapers grew their audience as they merged.

Partisan papers gave way to a brand of news that strived for objectivity. The profit motive mostly drove the change. To attract a mass audience, newspapers had to represent various points of view. This pushed some of the most opinionated citizens, particularly strong advocates for workers, to the fringes of mass discourse. Some advocates developed alternative media offerings. Others went mostly unheard or plied their craft directly in politics.

At the same, throughout much of the 20th century, the journalism workforce became more professionalized. Professional norms, that is the written and unwritten rules guiding behavior decided on by people in a given field, evolved. Many full-time, paid professional journalists stressed and continue to stress the need to remain detached from the people they cover so that journalists can maintain the practice and appearance of objectivity. Journalists emphasized objectivity in order to remain autonomous and to be perceived as truthful. The norm of objective reporting still strongly influences news coverage in newspapers as well as on most mainstream radio and television news networks.

That being said, the practice of maintaining objectivity is being called into question in our current hyper-partisan political media environment. Other strategies for demonstrating truthfulness require journalists to be transparent about how they do their work, about who owns their media outlets, and about what investments and personal views they may have.

At the heart of the ethical discussion for professional journalists is a sort of battle between the need to be autonomous to cover news accurately with minimal bias and the need to be socially responsible. Social responsibility in the study of journalism ethics is a specific concept referring to the need for media organizations to be responsible for the possible repercussions of the news they produce. The debate goes on even as more and more platforms for mass communication are developed.

Beyond advancements in ink-on-paper newspapers (including the development of color offset printing), technological developments have contributed to the diversification of mass media products. Photography evolved throughout the 20th century as did motion picture film, radio and television technology. Other mass media presented challenges and competition for newspapers. Still, newspapers were quite a profitable business. They grew to their greatest readership levels in the middle-to-late 20th century, and their value was at its high point around the turn of the 21st century. Then came the internet.

Stewing in Our Own Juices

With the rise of global computer networks, particularly high-speed broadband and mobile communication technologies, individuals gained the ability to publish their own work and to comment on mass media messages more easily than ever before. If mass communication in the 20th century was best characterized as a one-to-many system where publishers and broadcasters reached waiting audiences, the mass media made possible by digital information networks in the twenty-first have taken on a many-to-many format.

For example, YouTube has millions of producers who themselves are also consumers. None of the social media giants such as Facebook, YouTube, Instagram, Qzone and Weibo (in China), Twitter, Reddit or Pinterest is primarily known for producing content. Instead, they provide platforms for users to submit their own content and to share what mass media news and entertainment companies produce. The result is that the process of deciding what people should be interested in is much more decentralized in the digital network mass media environment than it was in the days of an analog one-to-many mass media system.

Media Consolidation

The process of making meaning in society — that is, the process of telling many smaller stories that add up to a narrative shared by mass audiences — is now much more collaborative than it was in the 20th century because more people are consuming news in networked platforms than through the channels managed by gatekeepers. A mass media gatekeeper is someone, professional or not, who decides what information to share with mass audiences and what information to leave out.

Fiction or non-fiction, every story leaves something out, and the same is true for shows made up of several stories, such as news broadcasts and heavily edited reality television. Gatekeepers select what mass audiences see, and then edit or disregard the rest. The power of gatekeepers may be diminished in networks where people can decide for themselves what topics they care most about, but there is still an important gatekeeping function in the mass media since much of what is ultimately shared on social media platforms originates in the offices and studios of major media corporations.

On social media platforms, media consumers have the ability to add their input and criticism, and this is an important function for users. Not only do we have a say as audience members in the content we would like to see, read and hear, but we also have an important role to play in society as voting citizens holding their elected officials accountable.

If social media platforms were only filled with mass media content, individual user comments, and their own homegrown content, digitally networked communication would be complex enough, but there are other forces at work. Rogue individuals, hacker networks and botnets — computers programmed to create false social media accounts, websites and other digital properties — can contribute content alongside messages produced by professionals and legitimate online community members. False presences on social media channels can amplify hate and misinformation and can stoke animosity between groups in a hyper-partisan media age.

Around the world, societies have democratized mass communication, but in many ways, agreeing on a shared narrative or even a shared list of facts is more difficult than ever. Users create filter bubbles for themselves where they mostly hear the voices and information that they want to hear. This has the potential to create opposing worldviews where users with different viewpoints not only have differing opinions, but they also have in mind completely different sets of facts creating different images about what is happening in the world and how society should operate.

When users feel the need to defend their filtered worldviews, it is quite harmful to society.

De-Massification

The infiltration of bots on common platforms is one issue challenging people working in good faith to produce accurate and entertaining content and to make meaning in the mass media. De-massification is another. Professionals working on mass-market media products now must fight to hold onto mass audiences. De-massification signifies the breakdown of mass media audiences. As the amount of information being produced and the number of channels on which news and other content can be disseminated grows exponentially, ready-made audiences are in decline.

In the future, it is anticipated that audiences, or fan bases, must be built rather than tapped into. One path to growing audiences in digital networks is to take an extreme point of view. Producers of news and entertainment information on the right and left of the political spectrum often rail against mainstream media as they promote points of view which are more or less biased. This kind of polarization along with the tendency of social media platforms to allow and even encourage people to organize along political lines likely contributes to de-massification as people organize into factions.

The future of some mass communication channels as regular providers of shared meaning for very large audiences is in question. That said, claims that any specific medium is "dead" are overblown. For example, newspaper readership, advertising revenue and employment numbers have been declining for about 25 years,

Media Consolidation

but as of 2018, there are still more than 30 million newspaper subscribers. Mass audiences are shrinking and shifting, but they can still be developed.

Convergence

As mass audiences are breaking up and voices from the fringe are garnering outsized influence, the various types of media (audio, video, text, animation and the industries they are tied to) have come together on global computer and mobile network platforms in a process called convergence.

It is as though all media content is being tossed into a huge stew, one that surrounds and composes societies and cultures, and within this stew of information, people are re-organizing themselves according to the cultural and social concerns they hold most dear.

According to one hypothesis, in a society dominated by digital communication networks, people gather around the information they recognize and want to believe because making sense of the vast amount of information now available is impossible.

This text covers several mass media channels including social media, film, radio, television, music recording and podcasting, digital gaming, news, advertising, public relations and propaganda because these are still viable industries even as the content they produce appears more and more often on converged media platforms.

What we see emerging in networked spaces is a single mass media channel with a spectrum of possible text, photo, audio, video, graphic and game elements; however, the sites of professional production still mostly identify as one particular industry (such as radio and recorded music, film, television, cable television, advertising, PR, digital advertising or social media). Some of these are "legacy" media that have existed as analog industries prior to convergence, while others originated in digital media environments.

For the foreseeable future, we should expect legacy media producers to continue to hold formidable power as elements of larger media conglomerates, which acquired many media companies as a result of industry deregulation. We should also expect audiences to continue to fragment and digital media start-ups trying to build audiences out of fragmented communities to be common even if they are difficult to sustain.

What this means for social structures and for cultural production is disruption, limited perhaps by legacy media traditions and corporate power.

Melding Theories

The world of mass media has witnessed the convergence of media content on digital platforms, the ability of individuals to engage in one-to-many communication as though they were major broadcasters, and the emergence of structures that allow for many-to-many communication. These developments force us to rethink how separate interpersonal, organizational and mass communication truly are.

From a theoretical standpoint, these are well-established approaches to thinking about communication, but in practice, certain messages might fit into multiple categories. For example, a YouTube video made for a few friends might reach millions if it goes viral. Is it interpersonal communication, mass communication or both? Viral videos and memes spread to vast numbers of people but might start out as in-jokes between internet friends or trolls. The message's original meaning is often lost in this process. In a networked society, it can be difficult to differentiate between interpersonal and mass communication. For our purposes, it will be helpful to consider the message creator's intent.

As a user, it is essential to realize the possibility that interpersonal messages may be shared widely. As professionals, it also helps to realize that you cannot force a message to go viral, although most social media platforms now engage in various kinds of paid promotion where brands and influential users can pay to have their content spread more widely more quickly.

Media Consolidation

We must also understand that advertisers treat digital communication platforms much the same way whether they appear to users to be interpersonal or mass media environments. Users can be targeted down to the individual on either type of platform, and advertisers (with the help of platform creators), can access mass audiences, even when users are intending only to participate on a platform for purposes of interpersonal communication.

Scholars are still working to define how these platforms mix aspects of interpersonal and mass communication. Here is one takeaway: If you are not paying to use a platform like Facebook, Twitter, YouTube (Google), Instagram or Snapchat, *you* are the product. It is your attention that is being sold to advertisers.

The Big Picture

Society functions when the mass media work well, and we tend not to think about the technologies or the professionals who make it all possible. Interpersonal communication can function with or without a massive technological apparatus. It is more convenient, though, to be able to text each another. When interpersonal communication breaks down, we have problems in our relationships. When organizational communication breaks down, it creates problems for groups and companies. But when mass communication breaks down, society breaks down.

Cultural Production

There is another way of looking at the mass media that needs to be mentioned after looking in some depth at the structural changes going on in and around the field of mass communication. Mass media channels are also huge engines of cultural production. That is, they make the entertainment that helps us define who we are as large and small groups of people. To quote from *Dead Poets Society*: "We read and write poetry because we are members of the human race, and the human race is filled with passion. Medicine, law, business, engineering, these are noble pursuits and necessary to sustain life. But poetry, beauty, romance, love, these

| 86

are what we stay alive for." If you replace "reading and writing poetry" with "creating culture," you get a sense of the importance of cultural production. We can define culture as a collection of our knowledge, beliefs and practices. In practice, culture it how we express ourselves and enjoy life's experiences.

In media, there are three main types of cultural works, those associated with "high" culture, popular culture and folk culture. (Some scholars discuss "low" culture, but it is argued here that "low culture" is just another way of describing the low end of pop culture.)

- High culture is arguably the best cultural material a society has to offer. Economic class often comes into play in defining what is "high culture" and what is not.
- Pop culture is the vast array of cultural products that appeal to the masses.
- Folk culture refers to cultural products borne out of everyday life identifiable because they usually have practical uses as well as artistic value. It is often associated with prehistoric cultures, but that is because the folk culture, pop culture and high culture of prehistoric peoples were often one and the same. Their best art may also have been an everyday object like a bowl or a basket or a doll or a mask. Don't confuse prehistoric art with modern folk art.

Modern folk art has the specific quality of trying to capture what is both beautiful *and useful* in everyday life.

Folk music tends to rely on "traditional" sounds and instruments. Topically, it focuses on the value of everyday existence. Folk music is often built around narratives that carry morals much the same way fairy tales do. Fairy tales are probably the best example of folk literature.

So much of the interpretation and the value of cultural production is culturally relative. This means that an object or work's value is determined by perceptions of people in different cultural groups.

Media Consolidation

In modern society, mass media often drive our perceptions. It is important to recognize that different cultures have different moral values and to acknowledge that some practices should be universally abhorred and stopped, even if they are partially or wholly accepted in other cultures.

The relationship between culture and mass media is complex; it is difficult to distinguish modern culture from how it appears in the various mass media. Culture in the developed world is spread through mass media channels. Just as society forms and is formed in part by messages in the mass media, so it goes with culture. Cultural products and their popularity can influence which media channels people prefer. Conversely, changes in media and ICTs can lead to changes in how we produce culture.

[...]

VIEWPOINT 5

> *"TV and movies fill the knowledge gaps with powerful images and stories that inform the way we think about different cultures."*

Netflix Can Use Its Media Power to Help Create Cross-Cultural Understanding

Paolo Sigismondi

In this viewpoint, Paolo Sigismondi explains how Netflix has been using its money and massive number of subscribers to develop content in countries beyond the U.S., which it then distributes on a global scale. Because Netflix is one of a few major media companies and has a large amount of influence in the media world, it has a significant amount of power in shaping the cultural landscape and determining what kind of media Americans are exposed to. Through introducing viewers to movies and TV shows from other countries, Netflix helps its subscribers get a more nuanced and less stereotypical understanding of other cultures. Paolo Sigismondi is a clinical professor of communication at the USC Annenberg School for Communication and Journalism.

As you read, consider the following questions:
1. According to this viewpoint, how has the way people are exposed to media entertainment changed in recent years?

"Netflix's big bet on foreign content and international viewers could upend the global mediascape – and change how people see the world," by Paolo Sigismondi, The Conversation, April 7, 2021, https://theconversation.com/netflixs-big-bet-on-foreign-content-and-international-viewers-could-upend-the-global-mediascape-and-change-how-people-see-the-world-156629. Licensed under CC BY-ND 4.0 International.

Media Consolidation

2. What does Sigismondi mean by the "glocalization of entertainment"?

3. According to Sigismondi, how could Netflix change the way viewers see foreign cultures and people?

As a kid growing up in Italy, I remember watching the American TV series "Happy Days," which chronicled the 1950s-era Midwestern adventures of the Fonz, Richie Cunningham and other local teenagers.

The show, combined with other American entertainment widely available in Italy in the 1970s and 1980s, shaped my perception of the United States long before I ever set foot in the country. Today, I call the U.S. home, and I have developed my own understanding of its complexities. I am able to see "Happy Days" as a nostalgic revival of an ideal, conflict-free American small town.

"Happy Days" was a product of Hollywood, which is arguably still the epicenter of the global entertainment industry. So recent news that the streaming service Netflix is opening an Italian office and will begin massively funding original local content with the intent of distributing it globally on its platform – following a strategy already launched in other European countries – struck me.

This could be a potentially game-changing move in global entertainment. And it might even change how the world perceives, well, the world.

Learning by Watching

I have explored the global media landscape from the privileged vantage point of Los Angeles for the past 15 years.

TV and movies are one way that people, as we go through life, make sense of the world, building on the archive of our personal experiences and opinions of other places.

Absent direct experience with a people or nation, we speculate on what we do not know. This process involves a variety of sources, including reading, Googling and accounts from somebody we trust. But often it is media that exposes people to other cultures, above and beyond our own.

TV and movies fill the knowledge gaps with powerful images and stories that inform the way we think about different cultures. If the media's messages have consistency over time, we may come to understand these as facts.

But media portrayals may well be inaccurate. Certainly, they are incomplete. That's because movies and TV series aren't necessarily meant to depict reality; they are designed for entertainment.

As a result, they can be misleading, if not biased, based on and perpetuating stereotypes.

For example, there is no shortage of Italian and Italian American stereotypes in American entertainment. From the award-winning "Godfather" saga to the less critically acclaimed "Jersey Shore" TV series, Italians are often depicted as tasteless, uneducated, linked to organized crime – or all three.

Media Is a Window to the World

But the way people are exposed to media entertainment is changing. Today streaming platforms like Netflix, Amazon Prime, Apple TV+ and Disney+ collectively have 1 billion subscribers globally.

Being a relative newcomer in producing original content, Netflix cannot rely on a large library of proprietary content to feed its 204 million paid members in over 190 countries, as legacy Hollywood players can. So it is increasingly creating original productions, including a number of non-English language originals from places such as Mexico, France, Italy, Japan and Brazil.

We might call this an example of "glocalization of entertainment" – a company operating globally, adapting its content to meet the expectations of locally situated audiences across the world.

This is already the modus operandi, for example, of many popular reality TV shows. "American Idol" is an American adaptation of Europe's "Pop Idol." "The X Factor," "Big Brother" and "Dancing with the Stars" have similarly international origins.

Now, however, glocalization comes with a twist: Netflix intends to distribute its localized content internationally, beyond the local markets.

It is not the global reach of Netflix's platform per se that would break down old stereotypes. French critics panned the American-produced, internationally distributed Netflix series "Emily in Paris" for its cliched, romanticized portrayal of the city.

Foreign TV executives must create shows for Netflix that both appeal to local audiences and have international potential, while remaining authentic in their portrayal of their country. If Netflix's Italian team thinks "The Godfather" is what international audiences expect from Italy, international audiences may tune in – but Italians won't.

To become truly international, Netflix would also have to foster the development of original local ideas not only in European countries with well-developed cultural industries but also in smaller countries and those with emerging entertainment industries, such as African nations.

Netflix's Opportunity—and Challenge

A side effect of this strategy could be that Netflix upends the traditional way that media informs our understanding of foreign people and lands by more accurately representing these places.

But that's a tall order, and it's not, of course, guaranteed.

Netflix's transformative potential comes from allowing local creatives to tell stories about their own cultures and then distributing them truly internationally. It will depend on the company's willingness to implement this strategy in a consistent, sustained, inclusive and thoughtful fashion.

Over time, widespread exposure to a diverse array of international media content might change the way people in the U.S. and worldwide think and feel about other cultures they have never, and may never, come into direct contact with.

All it takes is one click – one choice to watch, perhaps even unknowingly, a foreign-produced series.

The way Netflix works, using algorithms to suggest content as viewers make selections, can prolong an initial exposure to and interest in foreign content. Artificial intelligence meant to feed us more of what we like may end up a surprising force for change, making us rethink what we thought we knew.

Periodical and Internet Sources Bibliography

The following articles have been selected to supplement the diverse views presented in this chapter.

David Bloom, "Hollywood Huddle: Media Companies Headed to Bundles, M&A In 2024," *Forbes*, December 26, 2023. https://www.forbes.com/sites/dbloom/2023/12/26/hollywood-huddle-media-companies-headed-to-bundles-ma-in-2024/?sh=1cd5bdeb74f2/.

Arvyn Cerézo, "What Happens When Publishing Houses Merge?" Book Riot, November 23, 2022. https://bookriot.com/what-happens-when-publishing-houses-merge/.

Winston Cho, "Wall Street's M&A Sharks Are Getting Ready for a Feeding Frenzy of Hollywood Deals," *Hollywood Reporter*, September 6, 2023. https://www.hollywoodreporter.com/business/business-news/hollywood-deals-consolidation-1235582948/.

Constance Grady, "The Planned Penguin Random House-Simon & Schuster Merger Has Been Struck Down in Court," *Vox*, updated November 1, 2022. https://www.vox.com/culture/23316541/publishing-antitrust-lawsuit-merger-department-justice-penguin-random-house-simon-schuster.

Richard Howorth, "American Literature Loses Out to Consolidation," *New York Times*, August 11, 2022. https://www.nytimes.com/2022/08/11/opinion/penguin-simon-schuster-publishing.html.

Alex Kirshner, "The Publishing Industry Has a New Nightmare: Consolidation Was Supposed to Be Books' Biggest Threat. Is Private Equity Worse?" *Slate*, August 11, 2023. https://slate.com/business/2023/08/simon-schuster-kkr-private-equity-publishing-consolidation.html.

Nathan McAlone, "Please, Lina Khan, Don't Make Hollywood's Crisis Worse," *Business Insider*, August 25, 2023. https://www.businessinsider.com/why-lina-khan-wrong-about-hollywood-consolidation-market-structure-2023-8.

Media Consolidation

Agata Mrva-Montoya, "Is the Consolidation of Publishing Houses Good or Bad for Authors?," University of Sydney, August 15, 2022. https://www.sydney.edu.au/news-opinion/news/2022/08/15/is-the-consolidation-of-publishing-houses-good-or-bad-for-author.html.

Grady Rajagopalan, "The Threat of Record Consolidation: How Innovative Music Is Being Undermined by Corporate Interests," *Knight Time*, April 14, 2023. https://chsktr.com/5857/opinion/the-threat-of-record-consolidation-how-innovative-music-is-being-undermined-by-corporate-interests/.

Lillian Rizzo, "The Media Industry Is in Turmoil, and That's Not Changing Anytime Soon," CNBC, July 17, 2023. https://www.cnbc.com/2023/07/17/media-industry-turmoil-strikes-streaming-losses-ad-slump.html.

CHAPTER 3

Does Media Consolidation Damage the Economy?

Chapter Preface

The previous chapter took a look at the subtle and not-so-subtle effects of media consolidation on culture. In this chapter, the authors examine the economic results of media consolidation. The issues in many ways are similar to the ones discussed in the previous chapters. However, by looking at the situation through an economic lens, the authors here are able to shed some light on whether or not media consolidation is harming economies both local and national. In addition, these viewpoints look closely at the complex interplay of economics and policy behind media consolidation and its effects.

The author of the first viewpoint offers some economic and regulatory history. She explains that the original mandate of media companies was to offer a public service. That has changed, she says, so that now profit is the purpose of news divisions as well as entertainment divisions. She suggests a solution, but the impetus behind it will have to come from the public.

The next author in this chapter points out that monopolies can have some advantages, such as lower prices (sometimes) and a wider variety of products. Can these advantages of manufacturing monopolies translate to media conglomerates?

The next viewpoint considers the ways in which media consolidation impacts broadcast corporations. The data suggests that consolidation overwhelmingly benefits these corporations, but consumers may not have as positive of an experience.

The chapter closes with a thoughtful look at the pros and cons of monopolies and in the process offers a succinct lesson about the history of monopolies and efforts to rein them in.

VIEWPOINT 1

> *"In late October 2017, the Federal Communications Commission made it even easier for media conglomerates to focus on money-making."*

Turning News Divisions into Profit Centers Is a Bad Idea

Margot Susca

In this viewpoint, Margot Susca explains how news divisions of media companies went from being a public service to a money-making venture. Previous chapters have demonstrated how corporate ownership damages local news. Here we learn more about the economics behind that development. The viewpoint points to the Telecommunications Act of 1996, signed into law by former president Bill Clinton, as a major turning point in media consolidation. While it was meant to increase competition and innovation through deregulation, instead it has reduced competition through consolidation. Margot Susca is political economist and assistant professor in the journalism division at American University.

As you read, consider the following questions:

1. What was "the main studio rule"?

"Here's why your local TV news is about to get even worse," by Margot Susca, The Conversation, November 13, 2017. https://theconversation.com/heres-why-your-local-tv-news-is-about-to-get-even-worse-86443. Licensed under CC-BY-ND 4.0 International.

Media Consolidation

2. How did proponents argue that removing the local requirement would create more jobs? What was the counterargument to this?
3. How did deregulation harm rural residents more than others, according to Susca?

Considering the history of television news a few years ago, iconic anchor Ted Koppel declared that CBS' 1968 debut of "60 Minutes" forever altered the landscape of broadcast journalism: A news program drew enough advertising to turn a profit. As Koppel told it, "60 Minutes" showed broadcasters that news divisions could make money – which was a huge shift in how management executives thought of news, affecting both the quality and type of coverage broadcast over the publicly owned airwaves.

Until then, broadcast news in the U.S. had been a costly requirement media companies had to bear as part of getting permission to use the airwaves. "All of a sudden, making money became part of what we did," Koppel told the audience of a "Frontline" series called "News War."

In the decades since, news divisions have been held to the same profit-making standards as corporate media's entertainment divisions. Corporate owners slashed foreign bureaus as coverage remained focused on emotion and celebrity rather than public affairs.

In late October 2017, the Federal Communications Commission made it even easier for media conglomerates to focus on money-making. That was when the FCC abolished a World War II-era policy that was intended to force news broadcasters to be connected to – and accountable to – the communities their programming reached. My work as a political economist suggests that local broadcast media content is about to get worse, focusing even more on stories that can turn a profit for corporate headquarters rather than serving local communities. And the big companies that operate these stations are going to withdraw even farther from the communities they cover, threatening a key foundation of American democracy.

Connecting with Communities

The longstanding requirement, known as the "main studio rule," said television and radio broadcasters had to have local studios, where viewers or listeners could interact with and communicate with the people who were putting their news on the air. This was part of fulfilling the broadcasters' explicit obligation to use the airwaves to benefit society: As the Radio Act of 1927 put it, they had to operate in the "public interest, convenience and necessity."

That would help keep news decisions about schools, zoning, health, environment, emergencies and local issues connected to the community. It also helped encourage broadcasters to employ people who lived in the areas their signals reached.

In the decades since, the media landscape and technology both have changed dramatically. The FCC still assumes that broadcasters are local media because it issues station licenses in specific community areas. Yet the holders of those licenses are usually large conglomerates with centralized news operations sending homogenized programming out across the nation.

Advocates for eliminating the main studio rule – including the National Association of Broadcasters – note that most audience communications with media companies are online. They say that makes having a local physical office less important than it may once have been. Among the supporters of this view is FCC Chairman Ajit Pai, who was appointed to the commission by Barack Obama in 2012 and tapped to head it by Donald Trump shortly after his inauguration.

Pai also raises another common argument against the main studio rule: its cost. In October he wrote that the policy change will reduce burdens on media companies and let them improve audience service accordingly: "eliminating this rule will enable broadcasters to focus more resources on local

Media Consolidation

programming, newsgathering, community outreach, equipment upgrades, and attracting talent – all of which will better serve their communities."

The two Democratic members of the five-member FCC, Mignon Clyburn and Jessica Rosenworcel, dissented from their Republican colleagues' decision, objecting to the effects the ruling would have on local news. Clyburn wrote that the FCC's change "signals that it no longer believes, those awarded a license to use the public airwaves, should have a local presence in their community." Rosenworcel, for her part, wrote in a separate dissent: "I do not believe it will lead to more jobs. I do believe it will hollow out the unique role broadcasters play in local communities."

History has heard this argument before.

Promises of Deregulation

As the lesson of "60 Minutes" spread in the late 1970s and 1980s, news organizations and their corporate parent companies enjoyed massive windfalls, broadcasting content that was cheap to produce: It focused on thin happy banter between anchors rather than substantive hard-hitting reporting. At the same time, media conglomerates including Time Inc., NBC owner General Electric and Comcast began heavily lobbying Congress and regulatory agencies like the FCC to roll back decades of media policies meant to help foster educational and informational needs of citizens in a democracy.

They found success when President Bill Clinton signed the sweeping Telecommunications Act of 1996. Then-FCC chairman Reed Hundt declared that with the act, "We are fostering innovation and competition in radio." He said the new law would increase diversity in both ownership of broadcast stations and the viewpoints they present. And he said it would create a space for more competition in the telecommunications marketplace that would, ultimately, benefit consumers.

Media Consolidation Leads to Greater Profits...and More Layoffs

Big media providers are holding their own amid the current digital industry tsunami, but 21st Century Fox's unsuccessful $80 billion play for Time Warner signals a coming wave of media consolidation, Milestone Entertainment head Robert Tercek told the Merging Media 5 conference on Thursday.

"We're going to see a trend in the coming year where there's a lot more consolidation," Tercek said during a keynote address in Vancouver. With profits these days coming from pay TV, he pointed to Comcast proposing to acquire Time Warner Cable for $45 billion and AT&T in a deal to buy DirecTV for $48.5 billion.

More consolidation is expected, as Tercek pointed to profitable players like Time Warner, the Warner Bros. studio and HBO shedding jobs and costs to boost their share value or gird against becoming a takeover target. He said the recent layoff fever is defensive and reactive.

"Time Warner is doing extraordinarily well. They're having record profits, and strangely they're in the process of downsizing," Tercek said. Ditto at Warner Bros., which wants to stay out of Murdoch's clutches.

Before becoming a consultant, Tercek was formerly the president of digital at OWN Network, and had worked as senior vp digital at Sony Pictures Entertainment and as creative director at MTV.

"Those executives know that the minute Fox buys Warner Bros., all of those guys will hit the streets. The musical chairs will stop, as there's no more seats in Hollywood," he told conference delegates.

Tercek said Time Warner or Warner Bros. could yet be acquired by rivals other than Fox, and Discovery Communications and Scripps Networks Interactive are also likely takeover targets.

"Digital Media Guru Robert Tercek Talks Big Media Layoffs, Consolidation," by Etan Vlessing, The Hollywood Reporter, November 13, 2014.

Media Consolidation

But nine years later, a report from Washington, D.C.-based watchdog group Common Cause determined "the public got more media concentration, less diversity, and higher prices." Cable and phone rates didn't drop from competition, but skyrocketed with consolidation. Industry leaders' promises to add 1.5 million jobs turned into layoffs of more than 500,000 people. And Hundt himself 10 years later trumpeted not the improvements of service to the public, but rather the financial rewards reaped by corporations and their shareholders.

So now, more than 20 years after the act's passage, fewer corporations than before control a larger share of radio, broadcast and cable television in the United States. Many of those corporations have financial stakes in online media, too, meaning their reach and ideologies extend far beyond just television and the AM/FM dial.

The FCC's decision to roll back the main studio rule is yet another in a long line of policymaking and regulatory decisions that will further boost corporate media, not citizens.

A Pathway into the Future

By eliminating the main studio rule, the FCC has severed one of the last remaining ties between broadcasters and local communities. (Others, including rules about media companies' consolidation, are on the chopping block.) The body charged with ensuring media companies serve the public interest has opened the door even wider to treating news as a profit-motivated medium operated to benefit shareholders, rather than as a key element of American civic life.

Even before the FCC undid the main studio rule, the effects of the Telecommunications Act made local news more homogeneous and less diverse. This is particularly harmful for rural America, where just two-thirds of residents have regular broadband access at home – and only limited data services on their mobile smartphones. That means millions of Americans without regular internet access are relying on

Does Media Consolidation Damage the Economy?

broadcast television as their sole form of entertainment and information about their communities.

The real question for citizens is simple: Did deregulation work? Is the quality of broadcast news better today than it was 20 years ago? Will it improve if companies' legal and regulatory requirements are loosened?

All Americans know the answer. And so does the FCC.

VIEWPOINT 2

> "When markets are dominated by a small number of big players, there's a danger that these players can abuse their power to increase prices to customers. This kind of excessive market power can also lead to less innovation, losses in quality, and higher inflation."

Monopolies May Not Be All Bad

Áine Doris

The previous viewpoints have offered quite a bit of discussion about how media monopolies can potentially harm individuals, communities, and economies. But can they also have an economic benefit? In this viewpoint, Áine Doris looks at consumer products— not media—for examples of how monopolies can lead to better prices and more brand choice. In the industries this viewpoint examines, monopolies have actually led to more competition at the level of individual products. While big corporations subsume and attain ownership over smaller companies, it offers them more resources and greater efficiencies, which allows companies to spend less money on product research and development. Could this also happen with the big media players, such as Amazon, Facebook, and Google? Áine Doris is a freelance writer and editor in Barcelona, Spain. She specializes in business and finance.

"Do Monopolies Actually Benefit Consumers?," by Áine Doris, Chicago Booth Review, October 13, 2021. Reprinted by permission.

Does Media Consolidation Damage the Economy?

As you read, consider the following questions:

1. In this viewpoint, Doris is looking at the product level to analyze the impact of monopolies. What are the products of the media monopolies mentioned at the start of this piece—Amazon, Facebook, and Google?
2. What is the Herfindahl-Hirschman Index?
3. Do you think the lessons from manufactured goods can be applied to media? Why or why not?

Both Republican and Democratic politicians have been sounding alarms about market power in the United States, arguing that a few companies such as Amazon, Facebook, and Google have become too dominant. In July 2021, the White House issued an executive order and statement doubling down on antitrust law enforcement, with a promise to reign in "corporate consolidation" and "bad mergers" in the interest of US consumers.

A growing body of research supports this notion, pointing to a regulatory leniency over the past few decades that is driving concentration across US markets and segments. Stanford's C. Lanier Benkard and Ali Yurukoglu and Chicago Booth's Anthony Lee Zhang provide more support for this claim—in part. The researchers find abundant evidence of rising concentration at the broader market level, with more mergers, fewer players, and a rise in organizations with high market share.

But they find a different picture at the level of individual products, where more concentration has led to more competition.

Monopolies are generally considered to be bad for consumers and the economy. When markets are dominated by a small number of big players, there's a danger that these players can abuse their power to increase prices to customers. This kind of excessive market power can also lead to less innovation, losses in quality, and higher inflation.

Thus, US legislators have historically sought to limit the market power of large corporations. Three major antitrust laws have been

Media Consolidation

passed by Congress over the past century, all aimed at prohibiting price-fixing, preventing monopolies, and driving free competition as the rule of trade.

But the discussion about concentration has traditionally centered on the number of companies operating and competing in different segments, with less attention paid to the situation at the individual product level. When there are fewer players producing goods and services, does it follow that there are fewer goods and services to choose from—and therefore less choice for consumers in terms of prices?

The researchers analyzed newly available data from MRI-Simmons, a provider of attitudinal and behavioral US consumer insights, to reexamine and reassess trends in concentration in US product markets between 1994 and 2019. Indeed, they see divergent patterns emerge when it comes to companies and products.

In the area of household goods, for instance, corporate concentration has increased. Procter & Gamble and Phoenix Brands, among other larger companies, have systematically acquired the makers of brands such as Tide, Cheer, Ajax, and Fab in the detergents category.

And yet, at the level of individual product markets in detergents, as well as in personal hygiene products, shampoos, and toothpastes, concentration has declined and competition has increased, the researchers find. Over time, P&G's and Phoenix's conglomerated companies have not only continued to manufacture existing products, but they've also ramped up efforts to produce new brands.

Similar patterns can be seen in other markets including food and financial services, according to the study. Companies such as Nestlé, Kraft Heinz, and Visa dominate at the corporate level, but concentration has been dropping at the individual product level.

In total, the researchers looked at 337 consumer product markets using the Herfindahl-Hirschman Index—a standard measure of the size of companies relative to the industry they operate in—to assess concentration at the market and product levels over time. It's important, they note, that the study is limited to consumer markets and doesn't look at markets for labor or intermediate goods (components used to manufacture final products).

Industries with HHIs between 1,500 and 2,500 are considered moderately concentrated, with anything above 2,500 being highly concentrated.

"When you look at the distribution of HHIs at the local product level in consumer goods, concentration has fallen over time," says Zhang. "The median HHI fell from 2,256 in 1994 to 1,945 in 2019, so there has actually been a substantial improvement in competition in these individual product markets over time."

The researchers hypothesize that this effect could be driven by economies of scale and greater efficiencies in processes and operations as large companies consolidate their presence and integrate expertise and know-how from the smaller firms they acquire. Superior access to research and development and emerging technologies may also have a role to play in streamlining production and manufacturing—a benefit that seems to be making its way across conglomerates and their roster of owned brands and into the pockets of US consumers.

This has implications for US legislators concerned about rising concentration. To date, the understanding of the full dynamics at play within the US antitrust context has been incomplete, the researchers argue. "There is some subtlety required to understand the big picture and to see things through the lens of consumers, who are enjoying greater choice and more competitive product pricing from American manufacturers today than they were 20 years ago in certain markets," says Zhang.

VIEWPOINT 3

> *"Consolidation may be good for broadcast companies, but the cable companies that negotiate with broadcasters over the growing retransmission fees argue that it is bad for consumers."*

The Impact of Consolidation on TV Economics: It's Complicated

Deborah Potter and Katerina Eva Matsa

The economics of television, broadcast and cable, are very complicated. In this viewpoint, the authors sort out how media consolidation affects those already intricate economics. Consolidation allows TV stations to save on operations and offer retransmissions, which produce a significant amount of revenue. However, while media companies seem to benefit from consolidation, some argue that it negatively impacts consumers, with consumers ultimately paying more after consolidation occurs. Deborah Potter is a journalist, teacher, writer, and founder of NewsLab. Katerina Eva Matsa is director of news and information research at Pew Research Center.

As you read, consider the following questions:

1. Why are media companies eager to buy stations in politically competitive states?

"Impact of Consolidation on TV Economics," by Deborah Potter of Newslab and Katerina Eva Matsa, Pew Research Center, March 26, 2014.

| 108

2. In this viewpoint, Meredith CEO Stephen Lacy is quoted as saying that the money is in news. What does he mean by this?
3. What are retransmissions and why are they valuable?

The business benefits of consolidation are clear and unmistakable. Stations save on overhead by combining back office operations, including sales and engineering. They often move in together, cutting costs by sharing office and studio space. In Columbus, Ohio, for example, Sinclair's ABC affiliate, WSYX, is housed in the same building as the Fox affiliate, WTTE, owned by Cunningham but operated by Sinclair. The ABC and Fox affiliates in Springfield, Mass., owned by Gormally Broadcasting, share studios and live-broadcast trucks, branded with both stations' logos.

Another key benefit of consolidation is in the fast-growing revenue stream of retransmission fees. The more stations a company owns or operates, the more leverage it has to demand higher retransmission fees. "Scale matters just to even the level [of the] playing field," said Nexstar's Sook. "Without retransmission fees, we'd look more like the newspaper business rather than TV business."[1]

Bigger companies also have more clout to negotiate programming deals with networks or syndicators. "If you wanted a decent seat at the table talking to those guys, you had to have scale," said Barry Lucas, senior vice president of research at the investment firm Gabelli & Co. "Otherwise you were irrelevant and got pushed around."[2]

Station groups with the advantage of size have been pushing back, more than willing to let their stations go dark on distribution systems to press for higher fees, as CBS and Media General did in 2013. CBS reportedly won a 150% fee hike from Time Warner Cable to nearly $2 per subscriber in New York, Los Angeles and Dallas, more than double the industry average.[3]

Media Consolidation

The explosive growth of retransmission revenue was on display at the UBS conference late in 2013 as station group executives rolled out the numbers. Meredith Corp., which owns 13 local stations, reported that retransmission dollars had more than tripled in the last three years. Scripps CEO Rich Boehne said the fees had jumped from $11.7 million in 2010 to $42 million in 2013. Media General CEO George Mahoney said his company had enjoyed roughly a six-fold increase in retransmission revenue in four years—from about $12 million in 2008 to nearly $70 million in 2012.

U.S. Regulators Accuse Amazon of Illegal Monopoly

US regulators have sued Amazon, alleging that the internet giant is illegally maintaining monopoly power.

The Federal Trade Commission (FTC) said Amazon uses "a set of interlocking anticompetitive and unfair strategies" to push up prices and stifle competition.

Amazon said the lawsuit was "wrong on the facts and law, and we look forward to making that case in court."

It is the latest technology giant to be sued by US regulators.

The FTC's boss, Lina Khan, has had Amazon in her crosshairs for years.

In 2017, Ms Khan, then only 29, published a major academic article arguing the online retailer had escaped anti-competition scrutiny.

"With its missionary zeal for consumers, Amazon has marched toward monopoly," she said at the time.

Since her surprise appointment as FTC Chair in 2021, this case has been widely expected – and viewed as a crucial test of her leadership.

The dominance of a handful of powerful tech firms has led some US politicians to call for action that would promote more competition in online search, retail and social media.

However, the FTC under Ms Khan has had little to show for its strong rhetoric against Big Tech.

Stations keep only about half of that revenue–the rest goes to the networks in reverse compensation[4]–but the end result for station owners has been a substantial increase in the value of their broadcast properties.[5] "They're all saying, 'Oh my God! Retrans is a serious amount of money,' " said CBS president Les Moonves. "Stations, therefore, are much more valuable than they ever were."[6]

Retransmissions is only part of the reason TV stations have increased in value. Stations airing local news, whether they produce it themselves or get it from someone else, also

In February it lost its attempt to stop Meta from buying VR company Within.

And in July it lost an attempt to block Microsoft from completing its deal to buy the maker of Call of Duty.

There is pressure on Ms Khan to make at least one high profile complaint stick – and at the FTC they have high hopes for this case.

The agency, along with 17 state attorneys, claims that Amazon is a "monopolist" that stops rivals and sellers from lowering prices.

The regulator also alleged the internet giant's actions "degrade quality for shoppers, overcharge sellers, stifle innovation, and prevent rivals from fairly competing against Amazon."

However, Amazon says that if the "misguided" FTC lawsuit is successful, it would mean fewer products to choose from, higher prices, and slower deliveries for consumers.

The key part of the case involves consumers losing money – getting worse deals – because of the alleged monopoly.

US anti-competition legislation is complicated, but generally, prosecutors have to show companies have acted in a way that hurts consumers financially.

That isn't always an easy thing to prove when it comes to Big Tech, as many of their services are free – like Google's search engine or Meta's Instagram.

Earlier this month, a court battle began between Google and the US government, which has accused it of having an advertising technology monopoly.

"Amazon: US accuses online giant of illegal monopoly," by James Clayton and Tom Espiner, BBC, September 26, 2023.

Media Consolidation

pull in more advertising revenue. "All the money is in news," said Meredith chief executive Stephen Lacy, whose company is looking to buy more stations and is targeting those with top-rated newscasts.[7] News generates almost half the revenue for the average TV station, according to Radio Television Digital News Association research.[8] Under a typical joint operating agreement, a station that provides services for another station gets to keep about a third of that channel's advertising revenue.[9]

The potential for significantly higher ad revenue in election years also boosted stations' value. In the 2012 presidential campaign– the first one conducted after the Supreme Court's landmark 2010 *Citizens United* ruling –a record $3.1 billion in political ad revenue was spent in local television and many companies have reported huge increases in political ad revenue from the 2008 to the 2012 presidential cycles. At Scripps, for example, that revenue went from $41 million in 2008 to $107 million four years later, although at least some of that increase is due to Scripps' purchase of more TV stations.

As a result, broadcasters are looking to buy stations in politically competitive states. Nexstar cited "political advertising activity" as a major reason it bought two Citadel stations in Des Moines and Sioux City, Iowa—a crucial caucus state where presidential campaigns spend millions on TV ads.[10] It picked up two more Iowa stations in a separate deal.[11]

Wall Street's response to consolidation and the growth in retransmission fees has been to push broadcast stock prices considerably higher. Nexstar's stock value more than tripled in 2013, while Sinclair's more than doubled. Gannett's stock price jumped 34% the day it announced it was buying Belo.[12] "The broadcasting industry has developed a reputation for being a great generator of cash," said Michael Alcamo, president of investment banking firm M.C. Alcamo & Co.[13]

Expanding companies like Nexstar and Sinclair also reported sharply higher third-quarter revenue in 2013, bucking the expected trend of lower broadcast revenue in years without elections or

| 112

Olympic Games to drive ad spending. Nexstar revenue was up 40%; Sinclair's up almost 35%. With the exception of LIN Media, which also posted a double-digit gain, other broadcast groups reported losses or single-digit gains. The revenue from newly acquired stations accounted for most of the gains, but Sinclair said its revenues from stations it already owned were up 11% year over year, thanks to higher retransmission fees.[14]

Consolidation may be good for broadcast companies, but the cable companies that negotiate with broadcasters over the growing retransmission fees argue that it is bad for consumers. As large-scale broadcasters secure higher retransmission fees, "consumers ultimately foot the bill in the form of higher cable rates," said Matthew Polka, president of the American Cable Association, which represents small and medium-sized cable companies.[15] A 2013 report from the Federal Communications Commission found that the average monthly bill for expanded basic cable had increased, on average, about 6% a year between 1995 and 2012.[16] Currently, cable and satellite systems pay broadcasters only about 10% of what they have to give channels like HBO and Discovery, according to SNL Kagan, but the fees paid per subscriber are moving toward parity.[17]

Notes

1. Yu, Roger. "Retransmission Fee Race Poses Questions for TV Viewers." USA Today. Aug. 2, 2013.
2. Gollum, Rob, Edmund Lee and Andy Fixmer. "Sinclair on Prowl for More TV Stations as Deals Mount." Bloomberg. June 19, 2013.
3. Eule, Alexander. "Boom Time for Broadcast Stocks." Barron's. Sept. 21, 2013.
4. Reverse compensation is the practice of a commercial television station paying a television network in exchange for being permitted to affiliate with that network. The word "reverse" refers to the historical practice of networks paying stations to compensate them for the airtime networks used to run network advertisements during their programming.
5. Marszalek, Diana. "Ryvicker: Stations Losing $10.4 Billion in Retrans." TVNewsCheck. Sept. 18, 2013.
6. Eck, Kevin. "Moonves Says CBS Local Stations Worth More After Time Warner Battle." MediaBistro. Sept. 12, 2013.
7. Saba, Jennifer. "Meredith CEO on the Hunt for More TV Stations." Reuters. Dec. 9, 2013.
8. Papper, Bob. "Newsroom Staffing Stagnates." RTDNA.org. July 15, 2013.

Media Consolidation

9. Lovelady, Steve. "SSAs and JSAs – Some Unwritten Rules." CommLawBlog. March 26, 2012.

10. "Nexstar, Mission Buying 5 Stations for $103M." TVNewsCheck. Sept. 16, 2013.

11. "Nexstar to Pay $87.5M for 7 Grant Stations." TVNewsCheck. Nov. 6, 2013.

12. Eule, Alexander. "Boom Time for Broadcast Stocks." Barron's. Sept. 21, 2013.

13. Malone, Michael. "Street Takes Stock of Broadcasting Resurgence." Broadcasting & Cable. Oct. 7, 2013.

14. "Sinclair Posts Gain in 3Q Revenue." TVNewsCheck. Nov. 6, 2013.

15. "ACA Urges FCC Review of TV Station Duopolies." American Cable Association. Undated.

16. "Report on Cable Industry Prices." FCC.gov. June 7, 2013.

17. Marszalek, Diana. "Station Retrans Fees Up but ESPN Still King." TVNewsCheck. June 6, 2013.

VIEWPOINT 4

> *"A monopoly tends to set higher prices than a competitive market leading to lower consumer surplus. However, on the other hand, monopolies can benefit from economies of scale leading to lower average costs, which can, in theory, be passed on to consumers."*

Monopolies Have Both Advantages and Disadvantages

Tejvan Pettinger

In this viewpoint, Tejvan Pettinger explores both the advantages and the disadvantages of monopolies. In order to put the topic in context he draws on the history of both the United States and the UK. He argues that monopolies are not advantageous when they result in higher prices for consumers and too much political power for corporations. However, he says that there are positive aspects as well. Corporations often are able to spend less money on research, development, and production in monopolies through economies of scale, allowing for greater innovation. Furthermore, when an industry is a contestable monopoly—meaning another corporation could ostensibly enter the industry and serve as competition, corporations are incentivized to be efficient and keep prices low. Tejvan Pettinger is an author of several books on economics and an economics teacher in Oxford, United Kingdom.

"Advantages and disadvantages of monopolies," by Tejvan Pettinger, Economicshelp, October 4, 2020. Reprinted by permission.

Media Consolidation

As you read, consider the following questions:

1. As mentioned here, Standard Oil was the monopoly that prompted the first antitrust legislation in the U.S. What are today's biggest monopolies? What industries do they represent?
2. In what ways do monopolies influence the everyday life of the average citizen?
3. Why is it difficult for governments to regulate monopolies? Is that more difficult than it once was?

What are the advantages and disadvantages of monopolies? Monopolies are firms who dominate the market. Either a pure monopoly with 100% market share or a firm with monopoly power (more than 25%) A monopoly tends to set higher prices than a competitive market leading to lower consumer surplus. However, on the other hand, monopolies can benefit from economies of scale leading to lower average costs, which can, in theory, be passed on to consumers.

Disadvantages of Monopolies

1. Higher prices than in competitive markets – Monopolies face inelastic demand and so can increase prices – giving consumers no alternative. For example, in the 1980s, Microsoft had a monopoly on PC software and charged a high price for Microsoft Office.
2. A decline in consumer surplus. Consumers pay higher prices and fewer consumers can afford to buy. This also leads to allocative inefficiency because the price is greater than marginal cost.
3. Monopolies have fewer incentives to be efficient. With no competition, a monopoly can make profit without much effort, therefore it can encourage x-inefficiency (organisational slack.)

4. Possible diseconomies of scale. A big firm *may* become inefficient because it is harder to coordinate and communicate in a big firm.
5. Monopolies often have monopsony power in paying a lower price to suppliers. For example, farmers have complained about the monopsony power of large supermarkets – which means they receive a very low price for products. A monopoly may also have the power to pay lower wages to its workers.
6. Monopolies can gain political power and the ability to shape society in an undemocratic and unaccountable way – especially with big IT giants who have such an influence on society and people's choices. There is a growing concern over the influence of Facebook, Google and Twitter because they influence the diffusion of information in society.

In the late nineteenth-century, large monopolists like Standard Oil gained a notorious reputation for abusing their power and forcing rivals out of business. This led to a backlash against monopolists. But, in the Twenty-First Century, there are new monopolies which have an increasing influence on people's lives.

Advantages of Monopolies

1. Economies of scale. In an industry with high fixed costs, a single firm can gain lower long-run average costs – through exploiting economies of scale. This is particularly important for firms operating in a natural monopoly (e.g. rail infrastructure, gas network). For example, it would make no sense to have many small companies providing tap water because these small firms would be duplicating investment and infrastructure. The large-scale infrastructure makes it more efficient to just have one firm – a monopoly. Note these economies of scale can easily

Media Consolidation

outweigh productive and allocative inefficiency because they are a greater magnitude.

2. Innovation. Without patents and monopoly power, drug companies would be unwilling to invest so much in drug research. The monopoly power of patent provides an incentive for firms to develop new technology and knowledge, that can benefit society. Also, monopolies make supernormal profit and this supernormal profit can be used to fund investment which leads to improved technology and dynamic efficiency. For example, large tech monopolies, such as Google and Apple have invested significantly in new technological developments. However, this can also have downsides with drug companies able to charge excessively high prices for life-saving drugs. It also gives drug companies an incentive to push pharmaceutical treatments rather than much cheaper solutions to promoting good health and avoiding the poor health in the first place.

3. Firms with monopoly power may be the most efficient and dynamic. Firms may gain monopoly power by being better than their rivals. For example, Google has monopoly power on search engines – but can we say Google is an inefficient firm who don't seek to innovate?

Evaluation of Pros and Cons of Monopolies

- It depends whether market is contestable. A contestable monopoly will face the threat of entry. This threat of entry will create an incentive to be efficient and keep prices low.
- It depends on the ownership structure. Some former nationalised monopolies had inefficiencies, e.g. British Rail was noted for poor sandwich selection and some inefficiencies in running the network. However, this may have been partly monopoly power but also the lack of incentives for a nationalised firm.

Does Media Consolidation Damage the Economy?

- It depends on management. Some large monopolies have successful management to avoid the inertia possible in large monopolies. For example, Amazon has grown by keeping small units of workers who feel a responsibility to compete against other units within the firm.
- It depends on the industry. In an industry like health care, there are different motivations to say banking. Doctors and nurses do not need a competitive market to offer good service, it is part of the job. If we take the banking industry, the economies of scale in offering a national banking network are limited. If it was a merger of two steel firms, which has much higher fixed costs, the economies of scale may be greater. If two pharmaceutical firms or aeroplane manufacturers merged, there could be a good case to say they would use their combined profit for research and development.
- It depends on government regulation. If governments threaten price regulation or regulation of service, this can reduce the excesses of some monopolies.
- Environmental factors. A monopoly which restricts output may ironically improve the environment if it lowers consumption.
- It depends on how you define the industry. A domestic monopoly in steel may still face international competition – from foreign steel companies. Eurotunnel faces a monopoly on trains between the UK and France but it faces competition from other methods of transport – e.g. planes and boats.

Advantages of Being a Monopoly for a Firm

Firms benefit from monopoly power because:

1. They can charge higher prices and make more profit than in a competitive market.
2. They can benefit from economies of scale – by increasing size they can experience lower average costs –

Media Consolidation

important for industries with high fixed costs and scope for specialisation.

3. They can use their monopoly profits to invest in research and development and also build up cash reserves for difficult times.

Why Governments May Tolerate Monopolies

1. It is difficult to break up monopolies. The US government passed a lawsuit against Microsoft, suggesting it should be split up into three smaller companies but it was never implemented.

2. Governments can implement regulation of Monopolies e.g. OFWAT regulates the prices for water companies. In theory, regulation can enable the best of both worlds – economies of scale, plus fair prices. However, there is concern about whether regulators do a good job – or whether there is regulatory capture with firms gaining generous price controls.

Periodical and Internet Sources Bibliography

The following articles have been selected to supplement the diverse views presented in this chapter.

Zander Arnao, "Why Monopolies Rule the Internet and How We Can Stop Them," the *Gate*, January 4, 2022. http://uchicagogate.com/articles/2022/1/4/why-monopolies-rule-internet-and-how-we-can-stop-them/.

Helen Johnson, "The Unprecedented Consolidation of the Modern Media Industry Has Severe Consequences," the *Miscellany News*, April 29, 2021. https://miscellanynews.org/2021/04/29/opinions/the-unprecedented-consolidation-of-the-modern-media-industry-has-severe-consequences/.

Ted Johnson, "Vox Media Announces Layoffs Of 7% Of Workforce," *Deadline*, January 20, 2023. https://deadline.com/2023/01/vox-media-layoffs-1235228966/.

Timothy Karr, "Why NPR's Layoffs Are a Public-Policy Problem," *Free Press*, February 24, 2023. https://www.freepress.net/blog/why-nprs-layoffs-are-public-policy-problem.

Blake Montgomery, "The Amazon Publishing Juggernaut," the *Atlantic,* August 8, 2019. https://www.theatlantic.com/technology/archive/2019/08/amazons-plan-take-over-world-publishing/595630/.

Douglas E. Schoen, "It's Time to Break up Big Tech's Media Monopoly," the *Hill*, August 22, 2021. https://thehill.com/opinion/technology/568904-its-time-to-break-up-big-techs-media-monopoly/.

Derek Thompson, "What the Tech and Media Layoffs Are Really Telling Us About the Economy," the *Atlantic*, January 20, 2023. https://www.theatlantic.com/newsletters/archive/2023/01/what-the-tech-and-media-layoffs-are-really-telling-us-about-the-economy/672791/.

Sandeep Vaheesan and Tara Pincock, "Throwing the Book at Amazon's Monopoly Hold on Publishing," the *Nation*, January 8, 2024. https://www.thenation.com/article/economy/throwing-the-book-at-amazons-monopoly-hold-on-publishing/.

Media Consolidation

Ariel Worthy, "So Many Media Companies Are Laying Off Staff. What's Going On?" Houston Public Media, January 25, 2024. https://www.houstonpublicmedia.org/articles/shows/houston-matters/2024/01/25/475575/so-many-media-companies-are-laying-off-staff-whats-going-on/.

CHAPTER 4

Does Media Consolidation Increase Misinformation, Bias, and Polarization?

Chapter Preface

When a single corporation owns a large share of the media, that corporation and its leaders are in a good position to influence the coverage of the media companies they own. Does this mean media is necessarily biased toward the views of its owners? The authors in this chapter dig into that question. They also look at the recent rise of misinformation and conspiracy theories. These lies are being spread largely through social media sites that are owned largely by big companies (Facebook) or single, powerful individuals (X, formerly Twitter).

But all is not lost, according to the first viewpoint. This viewpoint points out that while media consolidation has resulted in much less local news coverage, local journalists have resisted pushes to make their coverage match the political viewpoints of their corporate bosses. Nonetheless, misinformation is still a huge problem.

The authors of the second and third viewpoints in this chapter take a close look at the main studio rule, which we heard about in a previous chapter, and other FCC regulations of broadcast companies that could potentially help rein in bias and misinformation by insisting that broadcasters serve the public rather than airing whatever will increase their bottom lines.

The last viewpoint shifts the focus to the issue of media consolidation in Australia and its impacts on political bias, though this is indicative of an issue impacting many Western countries. The author also discusses the ways the European Union (EU) is attempting to promote media diversity.

VIEWPOINT 1

> *"It appears that the standards and norms of journalism are alive and well among individual journalists and not easily compromised by one new owner."*

Local Journalists Resist Corporate Push to Run Biased Content

Lisa Marshall

In this viewpoint, Lisa Marshall argues that media consolidation does lead to the slashing of local news coverage but does not find that consolidation necessarily results in biased coverage. Large media companies buy up smaller media sources—in this case, local news channels—and coverage of local issues decreases as a result. However, during the acquisition of these small media outlets high journalistic standards are maintained, and research suggests that after consolidation news channels cover less party politics, steering away from the issue of political bias. Lisa Marshall is a writer, editor, and associate director of science storytelling for the University of Colorado Boulder.

"Media consolidation takes toll on local news but doesn't necessarily bias coverage," by Lisa Marshall, CU Boulder Today, October 20, 2021. Reprinted by permission.

Media Consolidation

As you read, consider the following questions:

1. This viewpoint offers what it calls "bad news and good news" for journalism. What is the good news and what is the bad? Does one outweigh the other?
2. The study reported on here found that rather than having a bias, Sinclair-owned stations simply covered less party politics. Is that a good thing? Why or why not?
3. According to this viewpoint, the corporate owners push stations to offer biased news programs, but local journalists resist. What tactics do the journalists use?

W hen big conglomerates buy up small news outlets, local news takes a hit. But the parent company may not influence the political agenda of its stations as much as some have suspected, finds a new CU Boulder study of TV goliath Sinclair Broadcast Group.

The paper, published this week in the journal *Electronic News*, analyzed hundreds of thousands of news stories from six stations over six years, using big data to ask the question: What happens to a station after Sinclair buys it?

The findings, the authors say, are both bad news and good news for journalism.

"This paper provides strong evidence that when a large corporation takes over a news station, the amount of local content produced diminishes. That's something to be concerned about," said co-author Chris Vargo, an associate professor in the College of Media, Communication and Information (CMCI). "But we did not see, at scale, the blatant issue manipulation some have suspected. We found no smoking gun."

Depleted Newsroom and Soaring Syndication

With 186 stations across 620 channels in 82 markets, Sinclair is among the largest owners of TV news stations in the country, reaching about 40% of U.S. households.

| 126

Some have criticized the rapidly-expanding company for stripping newly acquired newsrooms of resources, even though federal licensure mandates an emphasis on local coverage.

Sinclair has also been accused of imposing a top-down conservative editorial stance on its stations.

In one instance, the company required stations to run a weekly commentary called *Bottom Line with Boris* presented by a former senior advisor to President Donald Trump.

In March 2018, Sinclair required all stations to air a video of local anchors reading a script decrying the "troubling trend of irresponsible, one-sided news stories plaguing our country" and accusing other outlets for publishing "fake stories" and pushing their own "personal bias and agenda." Viral videos about the incident abounded.

"This company has a reputation for buying up companies and rapidly expanding, and also for its conservative spin. We wanted to ask, 'How does that really trickle down to affect local coverage?'" said co-author Justin Blankenship, an assistant professor at Auburn University.

To answer that question, the researchers utilized a massive database to analyze 346,586 news stories posted before and after six stations in Nebraska, Montana and California were acquired by Sinclair.

They found the amount of news content published overall steeply declined after a Sinclair acquisition—evidence the company may indeed be depleting its newsrooms of resources, the authors said.

For instance, at one Montana station, the average number of stories produced weekly dropped from 410 pre-acquisition to 160 post-acquisition.

For five out of six stations, local news content—which had already been on the decline—continued to slide. For one station that had been expanding its local news coverage, that expansion slowed after acquisition.

Media Consolidation

Meanwhile, syndicated content reposted from other stations in different markets continued to increase.

"The situation was already bad for local news and then it got worse" after acquisition, said Vargo, noting that one argument in favor of media consolidation is, via economies of scale, stations will be able to improve coverage. "There is no evidence these stations are being better taken care of under a conglomerate."

Journalism Standards 'Alive and Well'

The study did not, however, find a clear conservative shift in coverage once Sinclair took over.

Instead, it found that newly acquired stations covered party politics less.

"Some have assumed that if a conservative parent company took over, they would emphasize certain issues and deemphasize other issues. But we found no evidence that is happening at scale," said Vargo.

This finding is in line with other research on the so-called Sinclair Effect or what happens to stations under the company's ownership.

In comparing the content of news shows on Sinclair vs. non-Sinclair stations, Blankenship found that while those owned by the media giant tended to be more "cable-news style" with dramatic debates involving highly partisan sources, they did not carry a conservative political bias.

The infamous "fake news" script incident, while troubling, only happened once, Blankenship notes. And, anecdotally, some news directors have pushed back on must-run segments such as *Bottom Line with Boris*—deliberately airing them at times of low viewership.

"If you're looking for a silver lining here, It's this:," he said. "It appears that the standards and norms of journalism are alive and well among individual journalists and not easily compromised by one new owner."

VIEWPOINT

> "Media consolidation is therefore not neutral with respect to the content of news coverage."

The FCC Could Make Changes that Would Improve Local Coverage

Gregory J. Martin and Joshua McCrain

As in the first viewpoint, Sinclair Broadcast Group is the focus of this viewpoint. However, this viewpoint looks not only at the changes made when Sinclair or another large corporation takes over local stations, but why the corporation makes the decisions it makes, even when that is not what viewers want. In short, the fact that media conglomerates want to create content that will appeal to multiple markets, not just a local market, informs the type of content they create. Gregory J. Martin is assistant professor of political economics at Stanford Graduate School of Business. At the time of publication, Joshua McCrain was a graduate student in the department of political science at Emory University.

As you read, consider the following questions:

1. Why, according to this viewpoint, might Americans be less interested in coverage of local politics?

"The FCC's hands-off approach to media consolidation means that local news increasingly looks more like Fox News," by Gregory J. Martin and Joshua McCrain, London School of Economics, October 18, 2019. https://blogs.lse.ac.uk/usappblog/2019/10/18/the-fccs-hands-off-approach-to-media-consolidation-means-that-local-news-increasingly-looks-more-like-fox-news/. Licensed under CC BY NC 3.0.

129

Media Consolidation

2. Why might Sinclair provide coverage that its viewers do not want and that causes a drop in viewership, according to this viewpoint?
3. Would reinstating the main studio rule cause broadcasters to be more responsible in their coverage?

The American news media landscape – much like the American political landscape in general – has become increasingly nationalized and ideologically polarized over the past two decades. A handful of large national papers are growing readership and expanding their coverage, while nearly 1800 local newspapers have closed since 2004. On television, the trends are less steep but point in the same direction: local news viewership is in slow decline, while ideologically polarized national cable TV outlets gain viewers.

It's possible that these trends simply reflect adaptation by the news industry to changes in Americans' tastes for political information. In an age of increasing nationalization of elections, dedicated coverage of local politics may no longer be as valuable to citizens as it once was.

Our research investigated an alternative explanation: that these content shifts are driven not by outlets giving consumers what they want, but by changes on the supply side of the news market. The media industry experienced a wave of ownership consolidation that began in the 1980s but reached a crest in recent years. This consolidation trend was especially stark on television: by 2017, just five companies owned nearly 40 percent of full-power broadcast TV stations in the US.

We examined the consequences of an acquisition by the largest of these companies, the Sinclair Broadcast Group. In the summer of 2017, Sinclair purchased 14 local television stations previously owned by the Bonten Group. We examined what happened to the content and viewership of the local news broadcasts on these stations, and their competitors in the same media markets, before and after the acquisition. To do this, we collected a database of

| 130

roughly 7.4 million transcript segments from local news programs across the country, along with information about local news viewership at 743 local stations.

We found that the acquisition led to a roughly 25 percent increase in the share of news programming devoted to coverage of national politics at the acquired stations. This increase came largely at the expense of coverage of local politics, which declined by a similar amount. We also found that a measure of ideological "slant" based on the content of news segments shifted to the right at Sinclair-acquired stations following the acquisition, compared to other stations in the same market. Following the acquisition, news programs on Sinclair-owned stations looked more like Fox News and less like MSNBC than they had before.

Viewers' reaction to these changes was negative: Sinclair-acquired stations experienced a small drop in viewership following the acquisition. The shifts toward a righter leaning slant and more national politics coverage do not appear to have gained these stations additional viewers. It is thus hard to explain the changes in content that Sinclair implemented as being primarily driven by a desire to cater to viewer tastes.

Why did Sinclair implement these changes in content, if not to increase viewership and thereby its ad revenues? We posit an explanation driven by economies of scale in the production of news by a conglomerate owner. An owner of many stations operating in many markets like Sinclair can reduce production costs, perhaps dramatically, by substituting nationally-focused and ideologically unified content produced in a single studio for locally-focused and ideologically diverse content produced by many local journalists. Even if viewers don't like this change – and they appear not to – the cost savings could still dominate in Sinclair's thinking.

Media consolidation is therefore not neutral with respect to the content of news coverage. Consolidation changes the incentives of news providers, shifting coverage towards topics that can be distributed in multiple markets rather than those – such as local politics – that are market-specific.

Media Consolidation

Fake News Travels Faster than Real News

A study of 126,000 rumours and false news stories spread on Twitter over a period of 11 years found that they travelled faster and reached more people than the truth.

Researchers from the Massachusetts Institute of Technology also found that fake news was more commonly re-tweeted by humans than bots.

They said it could be because fake news tends to be "more novel."

The most common subject matter was false political news.

Other popular topics included urban legends, business, terrorism, science, entertainment and natural disasters.

Twitter provided its data for the research.

The firm told the BBC that it is already engaged with trying to devise a "health check" to measure its contribution to public conversation.

"False news is more novel, and people are more likely to share novel information," said Professor Sinan Aral, one of the study's co-authors.

While the team did not conclude that novelty on its own caused the re-tweets, they said false news tended to be more surprising than real news, which may make it more likely to be shared.

Prof Aral, Soroush Vosoughi and associate professor Deb Roy began their research in the aftermath of the Boston marathon bombing in 2013.

"Twitter became our main source of news," said Dr Vosoughi.

"I realized that … a good chunk of what I was reading on social media was rumours; it was false news."

The team used six independent fact-checking sources, including Snopes and Urbanlegend, to identify whether the stories in the study were genuine.

Their findings, published in the journal *Science*, included:

- False news stories were 70% more likely to be re-tweeted than true stories
- It took true stories around six times longer to reach 1,500 people
- True stories were rarely shared beyond 1,000 people, but the most popular false news could reach up to 100,000

Best Gossip

Psychology Prof Geoffrey Beattie from Edge Hill University in Lancashire, told the BBC there is a position of power associated with being someone who shares information that others have not heard before - regardless of whether or not it is true.

"People want to share information that is newsworthy - in some sense the truth value is less of a concern," he said.

He compared the spread of fake news with the sharing of gossip.

"The point about gossip is, the best gossip is juicy gossip - the last thing people are worried about is whether it is true or not," he said.

"It's whether it is plausible or not.

"We are saturated with news, so things have to be more and more surprising, or disgusting, to get attention."

"Fake news 'travels faster', study finds," by Zoe Kleinman, BBC, March 9, 2018.

Our results have strong implications for the regulatory oversight of mergers in the TV industry. One factor enabling Sinclair's rapid recent expansion was the Federal Communication Commission's (FCC) elimination of the "main studio rule", which required local news stations to maintain a physical studio in the broadcast area. The elimination of this rule increased the cost efficiencies of consolidation, encouraging a wave of mergers. Our findings document a cost of the current hands-off approach to cross-market consolidation.

Regulatory oversight has traditionally focused on measures of concentration defined at the local market level; for example, the FCC caps the fraction of stations in a single market that can be owned by the same company. Our analysis shows that such market-level concentration analysis is insufficient: the news content that would be provided by a TV industry consisting of a handful of national conglomerates would look very different than that provided by one comprising numerous single-market operators, even holding measures of market-level concentration fixed.

Media Consolidation

Given the importance of local news provision for the accountability of local elected officials, regulators should not neglect this effect of cross-market ownership consolidation on local news content. Current trends towards national consolidation in TV and other media ownership have worrying implications for the performance of local governments and for mass polarization.

VIEWPOINT 3

> *"The nationalization of news is clearly both a product of and an additional driver of the broader nationalization. The demand for national content is something that is not isolated from these broader trends, but I think it's also straightforward to suggest that it's continuing to drive the nationalization of politics when, again, we have fewer outlets covering local stuff."*

Local News Helps Prevent Polarization and Nationalization

Matt Grossman

In this viewpoint, the Niskanen Center's Matt Grossman interviews two academics—Daniel Moskowitz of the University of Chicago and Joshua McCrain of the University of Utah (coauthor of the previous viewpoint in this chapter)—about how the consolidation of local news TV stations into larger national media conglomerates has led to increased polarization and nationalization. Local news helps citizens learn more about local politicians, which encourages them to take a more nuanced approach to voting instead of voting straight Republican or Democrat at both the national and local level. The viewpoint also suggests that the political

"Can TV News Keep Politics Local?," by Matt Grossman, Niskanen Center, June 2, 2021, https://www.niskanencenter.org/can-tv-news-keep-politics-local/. Licensed under CC BY 4.0 International.

Media Consolidation

slant of companies like Sinclair Broadcasting Company impact how news is presented, increasing polarization. Matt Grossman is Director of the Institute for Public Policy and Social Research and a professor of political science at Michigan State University. He hosts the Science of Politics *podcast for Niskanen.*

As you read, consider the following questions:

1. What political impact does McCrain say Sinclair Broadcasting Company has had on news?
2. How does Moskowitz define nationalization?
3. According to data from the Pew Research Center cited in this viewpoint, what news is considered most trustworthy?

Most of the politics voters see are national and presidential. Local television news can help Americans learn about state and local politics, but it is threatened by nationalization. Daniel Moskowitz finds that local TV news helps citizens learn more about their governors and senators, encouraging split-ticket voting.

But Joshua McCrain finds that Sinclair broadcasting group has bought up local stations, increasing coverage of national politics and moving rightward. Local news coverage is in decline but offers one of the major remaining bulwarks against nationalization and polarization.

Matt Grossmann: Can local TV news keep politics local? This week on The Science of Politics. For the Niskanen Center, I'm Matt Grossman. Even though state and local decisions effect Americans everyday lives and livelihoods, most of the politics they see are national and elections are interpreted mostly through the president. So, how can Americans learn about state and local politics?

One of the major sources of information is local television news but it, too, is threatened by nationalization. This week I talked to Daniel Moskowitz at the University of Chicago about his recent *American Political Science Review* article, Local News, Information and the Nationalization of US Elections. He finds that local TV news helps citizens learn more about their governors and senators, encouraging split-ticket voting. But nationalization is decreasing this influence.

I also talked to Joshua McCrain of Michigan State and soon to be the University of Utah about his *American Political Science Review* article with Gregory Martin, Local News and National Politics. He finds that Sinclair Broadcasting Group has bought up local stations, increasing coverage of national politics over local politics and moving it, ideologically rightward. They both say local news coverage is in decline but offers one of the major remaining bulwarks against nationalization and polarization.

Moskowitz was trying to understand the role of media in nationalization of our politics.

Daniel Moskowitz: The paper really broadly set out to investigate whether the decline of local news sources, which is a trend that we've observed over the past couple decades, contributes to what political scientists are calling the nationalization of elections. And what we mean when we say the nationalization of elections is that the election outcomes across various state and local offices are increasingly tied to the presidential election outcome. So, we can observe this tightening of that relationship between the presidential election outcome and the state and local election outcomes at the constituency level, so state or district, at the county level, precinct level. But then the individual level phenomenon that's driving these aggregate trends is actually what we call straight ticket or straight party voting.

When voters vote for the same party across multiple offices, mechanically that's going to drive this aggregate relationship between presidential vote share and the vote shares of other offices. At the same time that we've had this period of electoral nationalization, there's been a huge upheaval in the news environment. In particular, the decline of traditional local sources of news, especially newspapers.

The paper is an attempt to get at whether this nationalization of the news helps to explain the nationalization of elections. In the paper, I focus on local television news to get at this broader question of the role of the media and changes in the media environment in the nationalization of elections. The empirical strategy that I use is the idiosyncratic nature of US television media markets. Because of exclusivity contracts between networks and stations and some FCC rules, these media market boundaries basically determine, for the most part, the stations to which a viewer has access. The boundaries are drawn based on where television signals traveled over the air in the 1950s.

So, they're kind of haphazardly drawn, they cross state boundaries. And that's a really important feature of these media market boundaries that this band states because it means that while most voters live in an in-state media market … that is, a media market comprised mostly of residents from their own state … some voters are sort of stuck in these media markets comprised of residents from neighboring state.

For instance, if we look at a couple of counties along the western Ohio border with Indiana, Van Wert county and Mercer county are adjacent to one another but Mercer county is located in the Dayton, Ohio media market while Van Wert county is located in the Ft. Wayne media market. And the Dayton media market is entirely in-state. The market only contains Ohio residents while the vast majority of the Ft. Wayne media market is comprised of Indiana residents. 93% of that market's population are residents of Indiana and only seven percent of the market resides in Ohio. As a result, the residents of Van Wert county get a lot of local television news about Indiana's office holders and not very much local news about Ohio office holders whereas Mercer county residents get lots of coverage about Ohio's office holders.

And as it turns out, access to this relevant local news coverage has really important implications on voter knowledge and voter behavior at the ballot box. The hypothesis I set out to test at the beginning of the paper is whether greater access to information about candidates down ballot from the presidential race allows voters to assess these candidates and these races separately from their judgment at the top of the ticket when they're voting in the presidential race. And what I find is that voters residing in in-state markets have greater knowledge about their senators and governor across a variety of measures of [inaudible 00:05:44] that are available in surveys.

In addition, voters residing in these in-state markets are about two to three percentage points more likely to cast a split president/senator ticket and they're about four to five percentage points more likely to cast a president/governor ticket. Given that the overall rate of split-ticket voting for these offices is about eight to nine percent during the time period that I'm looking at, these are quite large effects. It's about 25% of the baseline rate for senate races and about 50% of the baseline rate for governor races.

Matt Grossmann: McCrain was investigating what happens when a national conservative conglomerate, Sinclair Broadcasting, buys up stations.

Joshua McCrain: We find that Sinclair, which is this big conglomerate media ownership group that owns a bunch of local news stations across the country ... We find that when they buy a station what happens is the station that they buy spends a lot more time on national politics and a lot less time on local politics relative to other stations in the same media market. So, we're comparing stations in, for instance, Lansing, Michigan to other stations in Lansing, Michigan and not a

Media Consolidation

station in Michigan to a station in New York City, which is important for a lot of reasons.

We also find that the national politics coverage that Sinclair pushes out to their stations is slanted more to the right. Again, relative to other stations in the same media market. However, we find that even in that conservative media market, Sinclair-owned stations shift even further to the right. You can think of this as them becoming similar to Fox News, which we also show.

And then finally, we show that there is now viewership response; that there's no increase in viewership when Sinclair makes these changes. And if anything, there's a negative viewership response so they actually lose viewers after Sinclair acquires one of these stations and make those changes. And we think there's a lot of really important implications, as far as general questions that you as a voter might care about.

Matt Grossmann: Both research projects start from broader concerns about nationalization. Moskowitz wanted to explain how incumbents lost their advantages.

Daniel Moskowitz: So, I started just trying to hypothesize why incumbency advantage might have declined more recently. In other words, why incumbents seem to have greater difficulty actually separating themselves from their party so that they can perform better than a generic non-incumbent candidate on the ballot would. And the kind of thing that … The potential explanation that came to mind was the role of the media and changes in the media environment, which might make it more difficult for candidates to convey to voters that they're different and voters to ascertain differences between candidates and their parties.

And there has been a lot of political science and economics research on the effect of changes in the media marketplace, in particular, the focus has tended to be on the new entrants into the marketplace. So, a lot of papers on the effect of cable news, social media; those kinds of things. But I think there's been quite a bit less emphasis on the consequences of decline of the traditional sources of local news. There are important exceptions to that, of course, but I wanted to investigate whether there might be a link between the decline of traditional sources of local news and this decline in incumbency advantage, which is really a consequence of the nationalization of elections.

Matt Grossmann: McCrain says nationalization of politics and news reinforce one another.

Joshua McCrain: The nationalization of news is clearly both a product of and an additional driver of the broader nationalization. The demand for national content is something that is not isolated from these broader trends, but I think it's also straightforward to suggest that it's continuing to drive the nationalization of politics when, again, we have fewer outlets covering local stuff. So, any demand that still exists for local content is getting essentially washed out by just the lack of coverage.

I think, yeah ... I don't think it's possible to disentangle what's causing what here, but I do think it's definitely true that these economics, especially in local TV but, again, this is relevant for newspapers, are exacerbating it or potentially speeding it up. And some of this is actually a product of the regulatory environment. And you could imagine regulatory changes or revisions to previous regulatory regimes that would potentially produce incentives for media producers to spend more time on local politics.

That's not going to solve these problems but it might slow it down or it might perhaps facilitate some lower-level demand that currently exists for local coverage by producing economic incentives for the actual media outlets to cover it.

Media Consolidation

Matt Grossmann: Indeed, Moskowitz says nationalization and polarization seem to go together.

Daniel Moskowitz: It certainly seems to be the case that the nationalization of elections and partisan polarization are sort of inextricably linked and they certainly reinforce one another in the sense that with nationalized elections, candidates have little reason to even try to separate themselves from their party because they don't kind of get that electoral reward for doing so if voters are just casting straight ticket votes anyway. At the same time, when candidates within the same party aren't trying to separate themselves from their party and they kind of adopt nearly identical policy positions, voters have less reason to cast a split to get that ballot and defect. While we don't know which one's causing what or to what degree one is causing the other versus the other causing the other, I think we have a pretty strong sense that these things are very much intertwined and that they both do kind of reinforce one another. And so it's tough to imagine in the near term what could either disrupt nationalization or polarization.

Matt Grossmann: [inaudible 00:12:14] finds local news is disappearing overall.

Joshua McCrain: What we are going to see less and less of, and the baseline for this was already pretty low, is any coverage about the state legislature, city stuff, school boards, this level of politics that actually takes some people with on the ground knowledge that are going to do investigative reporting, have their relationships, and actually it's costly to do this, this is going to be decreasing and decreasing. It's already going away in newspapers. And in fact, some states don't even really have state level reporters anymore. I have a friend who has been a reporter for the *Atlanta Journal Constitution* for I think almost two decades, and he used to have essentially one beat, which

| 142

was state-level investigative reporting about the legislature. And now he's, I think he told me last year, he's got nine different beats. So he's now forced to spend his time covering all of these things. And that's a trend that's going to be ongoing. And I don't think that that's going to change necessarily. And that's going to have really bad implications for accountability across the board if people just don't know what's going on.

Matt Grossmann: But local TV news is still the most widely watched.

Joshua McCrain: What we find regularly early from pollsters such as Pew is that local news, especially local TV news is, is regularly one of the most trusted sources of news. It has viewership more than the aggregate total of cable news viewers. So back when we wrote this paper, it was around aggregate 25 million viewers per night and across people that consume. It's generally, again, like I said, one of the most trusted sources of local news. The majority of the content in a local news broadcast is not about politics necessarily. It's about the kind of stuff you would expect, crime, it's about local sports. It's a lot of weather coverage. So that kind of predominates the coverage, which is why it's fascinating that we find such big changes to the content when Sinclair buys these stations where they'll shift the relative amount of time spent on local news. For instance, they decrease the amount of time spent on local news by 25% relative to, again, other stations in the same market.

So local news is very kind of homogenous in a lot of ways across the country. It's what you would expect. However, that's what makes Sinclair's business model kind of interesting is that they started to push out these, these nationally produced segments that are very similar to what you would find on Fox News. And so now local stations would start showing these very strong opinion style segments with very strong political

Media Consolidation

slant, which is different than really we had seen previously in the local news market.

Matt Grossmann: Moskowitz agrees local news is overall in decline, but still reaches a lot of viewers.

Daniel Moskowitz: News consumption has become substantially more nationalized simply because of the decreasing availability of local sources of news. Newspaper circulation has declined by over 40% from the early 90s. Advertising revenues for newspapers have plummeted. In turn, newspapers have reduced their staff substantially. Over the past decade, the audience for late night, local television newscasts have declined by about 30%, which is a substantial decline, but it's actually relatively complicated to assess the degree of this decline in local TV news consumption because there are actually more hours of local TV news on the air than there used to be. So even if the audience for a specific time slot and the local late night time slot is traditionally the most watched time slot for local TV news. So even if that audience for that specific time slot has declined, it's not clear how much overall consumption has declined if at all, just because there's so many more hours of local television news on the air than there used to be.

In the paper, I cite some data from Nielsen, which is a company that measures television audiences, as well as other media audience and reach. And they note that in the first quarter of 2017, about 40% of individuals ages 25 to 54 watched local TV news in an average week and that these viewers watched on average about two and a half hours in that week. So local TV news, despite some declines in their audiences, still have a really broad reach. One thing that is worth considering is that there likely is a relationship in the quality of the local television news coverage and the presence or the strength of the presence of other local media in that market because television stations often amplify the reporting of, for instance, newspapers, and they rely on newspapers and other sources of media to do a lot of the original reporting that they then amplify.

Matt Grossmann: State lines allow Moskowitz to understand the effects of local TV news that crosses boundaries.

Daniel Moskowitz: The focus, I guess, on the out of state media markets isn't because I'm interested in those residents per se. It's just because they offer the composition of these media markets and whether they're comprised of residents of a neighboring state versus residents of that same state gives kind of a nice source of variation in the emphasis that stations in that market place on each state's office holders and the level of coverage they provide for each state. So the key sort of strategy in the paper is to compare voters in the same statewide electoral setting. So I use something called state by year fixed effects, which allows this within state and within year comparison, which can hold constant the candidates, the electoral rules, just as many features of that electoral context as possible.

But one thing that's different across these residents of different media markets is how much coverage about their governor and their senators based on whether they live in an in-state or out of state media market. About 20% of counties are located in an out of state media market in which less than 50% of the market's residents are in state. And about 43 states have at least one county located in out of state market. So these are pretty widespread, even if the vast majority of the population does not live in and out of state media market, just kind of by definition. Those voters who reside in the media markets that are almost entirely out of state get almost no coverage of their state's office holders. They get very little coverage. In comparison, residents of an in-state market are expected to get about an additional 1.5 mentions of their governor per hour of coverage and they get about an additional 0.5 mentions of each of their senators per hour of coverage.

Media Consolidation

So these are non-negligible differences, but there's just a greater level of coverage of governors and senators, which maybe isn't too surprising if you're someone who watches local television news. You definitely notice higher levels of coverage about the governor than you do about senators.

Matt Grossmann: Being in an in-state media market gives you a lot more state information.

Daniel Moskowitz: Being located in an in-state market increases the ability of voters to correctly recall the party of their senator by about nine percentage points, and their governor by about 11 percentage points, which are large and important differences between these residents. But one might be suspicious that it could just be that people who reside in these out of state media markets are different in certain ways than residents of in-state markets. And these differences, perhaps, for instance, they maybe have differences in educational attainment or other demographic characteristics, and that could explain the differences in knowledge. But when I look at whether access to in-state television is associated with greater national political knowledge, for instance, knowing which party controls the House and which party controls the Senate, I don't observe differences across various measures of national knowledge. And that seems to indicate that the differences in knowledge about senators and governors are then likely due to in-state television rather than differences between residents of in-state markets and out of state markets.

Matt Grossmann: And it does not seem to be an effect of television advertising.

Daniel Moskowitz: A big threat to inference in the paper is that the people who reside in these in-state markets not only get access to more relevant local television news about their

| 146

state's office holders, but they also get exposed to a lot more television campaign ads run by these candidates in these races, because it's not a very efficient use of campaign funds to air ads in media markets in which 90% plus of the market resides in a state that isn't voting in your race. So they tend to air their ads in in-state markets because they're reaching more voters doing that and it's a smarter use of their campaign funds to do so. But that means that there's another difference in the sort of media exposure that isn't due to news, but is instead due to television ads. And that could explain the differences both in voter knowledge- [inaudible 00:22:00], and that could explain the differences both in voter knowledge and in split ticket voting that I observed.

So what I do is I try to look at differences in voter knowledge for office holders who aren't running for reelection concurrent to the survey being administered for the data that I'm using. So I look at senators and governors who ran for election in a previous election cycle, and as a result, they are not likely to be airing ads on television. And what I observe is a similar size effect of in-state television on voter knowledge, which is strongly suggestive that the differences in voter knowledge are due to local television news rather than campaign ads since there aren't campaign ads being aired during that period of time.

Matt Grossmann: Nationalization of politics may not be done yet, but local news is an important break.

Daniel Moskowitz: If we look at kind of over time trends in ticket splitting from the ANES because the ANES kind of gives us the longest time trend in which we can measure split ticket voting for president/senator and president/House, those rates of split ticket voting were above 20% in the 1970s and '80s. And they started to really decline in the '90s, and now in 2012 and 2016, they're at about 8% or 9%. that's based on the ANES as

Media Consolidation

well as the CCS. They yield pretty similar estimates with the rate of split ticket voting.

These are obviously, like 8% to 9% is a pretty low rate. Could they go a bit lower? Probably, but there isn't too much room for them to go lower. With that said, the thing to keep in mind is that these are the overall rates, and so there are certainly really important exceptions to the kind of low split ticket voting.

So for instance, in 2012, Obama, obviously the Democratic candidate for president, got about 35% of the vote in West Virginia, and Joe Manchin, the Democratic candidate for the US Senate, got 61% of the vote, which implies an enormous rate of ticket splitting that occurred in West Virginia.

And that's obviously one of the more extreme examples, but there are several others indicating that, at the very least, it's not impossible for an elected official to kind of have their own personal brand that's distinct from the party brand, even in our present very nationalized context. We can also think about the handful of Republican governors in blue states that are quite popular, like Charlie Baker and Phil Scott and Larry Hogan.

My paper was based on data from 2012 and 2016 in which we were in this kind of highly nationalized setting. And so I think even in that setting, that I observed these effects based on kind of exposure to information and in a hyper polarized context, that there are these effects of information on voter behavior. It tells us that like it's still going to be important going forward, that voters still process information that they can get and they still use that to make decisions at the ballot box.

So I think the story will continue and it's just going to sort of depend on the degree to which local sources of news remain sufficiently prevalent so that voters can get information.

Matt Grossmann: You might think nationalization is demanded by viewers, but McCrain says that's only part of the story.

Joshua McCrain: We accept that there is a demand driven amount of national politics coverage. There's a demand driven amount of slant. And what I mean by demand is that the consumers in a media market want it, so then the media producers, these stations produce it to match what the consumers want. When Sinclair was asked about our research, this is what they said essentially, is that, "Look, we aren't doing anything. And if anything is changing, it's because we're filling in this gap of what viewers want."

So that's certainly possible that that's the case and we don't discount that, however, again, we still find that relative to stations in the same media market, we're still seeing these shifts. So it can't purely be explained by demand unless you are going to believe that every station that's in a media market that had a station acquired by Sinclair was just not realizing these things. And then, even if that was to be the explanation, we would also expect to see a viewership response, which we don't see.

So I don't think you can explain this purely by nationalization and demand. However, that being said, the political content of these stations across the country is strongly covering national politics, especially during this era that we're studying which was dominated by Trump, and that's what people were interested in, but you do see some variation across the country in how much time is spent on these things. A lot of it's predicted by whether or not there are other things going on, such as natural disasters. So we saw a lot of stuff on the fire coverage and hurricanes, stuff like that, crime. So there is variation, but it's hard to disentangle this with these broader trends towards nationalization that we see in American politics.

Matt Grossmann: He does see economic incentives to nationalize local TV news.

Joshua McCrain: So the economics of local news have changed substantially in the past couple of decades. This is definitely true

Media Consolidation

in local television news, as well as newspapers. So essentially what's become easier, and this was sort of accelerated during the Trump administration when they had a very friendly FCC, is that it became easier and more effective for these big nationwide conglomerate owners of which Sinclair is as a perfect example, but there are others, to essentially buy up stations across the country and then centralize the production of some content and then push it out to their affiliates.

So the idea here is that if a media group owns a bunch of stations in a bunch of different areas in the country, it's going to be costly for them all to do local reporting, which involves a lot of on the ground work, it involves actual reporters instead of just on-air personalities.

So what Sinclair has done is that they've basically cut a lot of that local investigative reporting and replaced it with this centrally produced content, which is clearly a cost saving mechanic, right? It's just much more cost efficient to do this. And again, I want to emphasize that this was something that was facilitated by changes to FCC rules that were specifically designed in favor of these big conglomerate owners to do these sorts of things, which in the past would have either been prohibited or been much more costly.

So just for an example, the FCC got rid of this rule called the Home Studio Rule, which said that a local news station had to have a physical broadcast building in the media market in which they exist. So the FCC got rid of that rule saying this was sort of anachronistic in the era of internet when you can be anywhere and get local news on anything. And maybe there's some truth to that, maybe there's not, but again, it's one of the many things that's been kind of a more friendly regulatory environment for these big media conglomerates.

So I want to circle back though to what we find vis-a-vis these economic rationale. So for Sinclair, you would have to believe that the reason that they're willing to make these changes, right, to the content, especially again, relative to other

| 150

stations in the same media market, is they think that they can make money off of these changes. And probably the biggest indicator that they are generating more revenue is an increase in viewership. And this is what they've, again, themselves suggested in interviews about our research is that this is what's going on, is they're getting these viewers in who want this kind of content.

We find zero viewership response, and if anything, we find negative viewership in response to a Sinclair acquisition of a channel. So this is incoherent with this demand driven explanation. If they're losing viewers when they make these changes, then what's going on? I mean, there are two explanations. One is what I just talked about, where there's a cost saving mechanic of centralizing production which makes it cheaper to do these things, and that kind of covers the difference between the viewers that they're losing.

Another one is that, and this is partly a feasible explanation because Sinclair is so overtly political, they're a very obviously right wing organization and their owners are strong Republican supporters, so another explanation is that they're willing to eat some of the financial costs of making these changes in order to gain some sort of persuasion and ability to change political outcomes through the style of their content in the same sort of way that Fox News is.

Matt Grossmann: Local news still matters, but it's difficult to make sustainable.

Joshua McCrain: There's a lot of assumed demand that's sort of latent and out there for local news, right? And the idea is that the business model has just not sort of adapted to making it a financial thing that can exist and sort of produce these public goods that we want out of local news, right? There's all of this great research that shows that there's all these negative effects when local news goes away, there's less accountability, people have less knowledge about politics. I think you're talking to

Media Consolidation

Dan Moskowitz who's shown a lot of this. Eric Peterson at Texas A&M has a lot of great research on what happens when there are cuts to local newspapers.

I think what underlies this is this question of whether or not we can even really have a profitable local news industry that's not propped up by essentially nationalized political content and it actually invests in reporting.

I think that there is some demand for local news. In general, we see people kind of finding it in these other outlets, especially the internet, such as Facebook, Next Door, those sorts of things, but that's not really news. It's not reporting. That's just events that happen, so you lose the context.

Matt Grossmann: Conglomerates like Sinclair might matter for political behavior and information as well.

Joshua McCrain: I want to emphasize though that Sinclair here is not necessarily unique, especially recently. So what we think is unique about Sinclair is sort of what Greg and I find, in that there's a slant, there's a change in slant to the coverage, but the business model of Sinclair of nationalizing this production of content and then distributing it to local affiliates, it's not obvious that, or it shouldn't be the case that that's unique. That's a very straightforward economic incentive.

So there's a couple pieces of research that I think generalize a little bit beyond Sinclair in this realm. So the [inaudible 00:32:41] paper is a little bit more about Sinclair, in which he actually finds that a Sinclair acquisition of a media market sort of has these, I would say moderate to minor persuasive effects on people's perceptions of Barack Obama, but it doesn't really find that they have any sort of effects on people's behavior beyond that.

So on people's behavior, beyond that, especially in the national political universe, which I think makes sense. Like the people who are going to be persuaded to vote for or against

Trump, I don't, based on local news content, I think that's a very, very marginal person.

So I think that makes a lot of sense. There's another paper that shows that by Nicola Mastrorocco and one of his coauthors that shows that Sinclair acquisition, because they cover less local crime, that this actually affects the crime clearance rates in a municipality that's within a district, or within a media market and which Sinclair buys a station.

So there's a lot of evidence like this too, where the content and the informational content of broadcasts is actually going to affect behavior. So what Greg and I are working on now is the idea is it's like it's not going to be national political behavior. It's not going to be whether or not people are going to vote Democrat or Republican, or for Trump or against Trump. It's going to be the effect of Sinclair, or less knowledge about local politics and more knowledge about national politics. It's going to be the effect that you see in local elections.

So these are already low salience elections. The accountability mechanism between voters and local politicians is pretty weak as it is when you don't know who these people are. So what we're looking at, and what we're finding is that, in these local elections, when any of the major conglomerate owners, not just Sinclair, such as Tribune or a Media General, there's a number of other ones, that voters have less knowledge about local politics. And this affects their behavior.

So what you see is, in these local races, the races become less competitive. There's a bigger incumbency advantage, those sorts of effects. And this is coherent with existing research on media and accountability.

And I think this is probably going to be the biggest source of new research on the changing media economics, is these informational effects, these informational mechanisms, especially in areas where there's already really low knowledge about who's running and what these people are doing in office.

Media Consolidation

Matt Grossmann: Moskowitz agrees that rules changes may move us toward more nationalized news.

Daniel Moskowitz: The FCC removed what's called the Main Studio Rule in 2017, which used to require every station to have a physical studio in the community where the license was issued, or near the community where the license was issued. The FCC also in effect raised the cap on the national audience reach of a single owner. And they reduced restrictions on media consolidation within the same market area.

And all of these things make it easier for a single entity to basically buy up lots of stations across the country and pipe in nationalized programming to stations around the country. To the extent that these trends continue, and that would suggest that the local aspect of local television news will not really be distinct from national programming. And we might not observe the patterns that I observe in the paper going forward.

Matt Grossmann: Increasing nationalized partisan media might change elite and public behavior, says McCrain.

Joshua McCrain: I think there's a feedback loop here. There sort of has to be. I think there's a good amount of evidence from a large body of research and media in politics that once people become attuned to partisan political media, like this is what they try to select into, especially congenial media, so media that aligns with their prior beliefs.

So I think the Sinclair case is an interesting one here where, if people are watching local news, maybe they don't necessarily have strong priors for partisan media, but now they're exposed to very politicized media almost overnight when Sinclair buys these stations.

So now they might select more and more into watching that. And you start this feedback loop where they then pursue more partisan outlets, et cetera. And then I think this must feed into elite behavior.

So people in these media markets, when this is what they are now being told, they need to worry about. In the Sinclair case, for instance, illegal immigration or whatever political story is arguably not salient to the local context is now something that they're just being shown nightly. This is something that must feed into elite behavior. This is what state level local politicians are now getting calls about.

And this is something that they know that their voters care about, so they must be incentivized to talk about it, or to create stories about it, to introduce bills in the state legislature about something that is insane from an actual local level. Like I'm a North Carolinian so I think of the Sharia Law Bill, stuff like that, where it's clearly not relevant, but it's something that's easy to get attention to.

And I think this would be a really interesting avenue for additional academic research is to actually look at the behavior of locally elected leaders or state officials around the changes in the media environment.

Matt Grossmann: Moskowitz is now looking at whether local TV news helps ideological voting.

Daniel Moskowitz: I have another object that I'm working on related to local television news. And it's actually trying to get at whether voters are better able to engage in ideological voting based on whether they have access to in-state television. And by that, I mean, are voters more likely to reward office holders for engaging in moderate behavior in office and punish officers for engaging in extreme behavior in office?

So some of that, when I presented this paper or gotten feedback on the paper that we talked about today, a lot of people had questions about, okay, split ticket voting is interesting, and it helps to explain this interesting phenomenon of the

Media Consolidation

nationalization of elections, but what are the implications for accountability, and voting, and whether voters are holding officials accountable for the way they're behaving in office in a way that we think makes sense with different models of politics that we have.

And so, this next project, hopefully, will get at that in a way that will interest scholars and help us understand better the way voters are engaged in the split ticket voting, and whether it matches up with the behavior of office holders during their previous term.

Matt Grossmann: And McCrain is working on additional work on media and politics.

Joshua McCrain: We're almost done with this paper on the effects in local elections, especially state legislative elections. We're working on, myself and Eugene Kim, and [inaudible 00:39:47] working on a paper on dynamic media bias and cable news broadcast.

So for instance, when Fox becomes more conservative over time, how does MSNBC respond? Do they try to become more liberal to capture the audience that's pushed away, or do they shift slightly more to the right as well to mirror this latent demand? So that's something that we're really interested in.

The other thing I'm really interested in, and I've started some conversations on working on this with some people is, what is the political behavior response to Sinclair ownership? So when people are now exposed to Sinclair, are they more prone to develop attitudes of racial animus or a xenophobia, because they're now imagine you been shown these nationally produced broadcasts in your local channel about how you got these caravans at the border who are going to come threaten your livelihood and your health.

And you must imagine that that has effects on people's attitudes towards these thing, when there was no other way

| 156

they were really going to view this, unless they were already predisposed to those positions because they were already consuming Breitbart or Fox news.

So those are some of the big things that I'm interested in. I also really think that this research that Dan is doing on the political knowledge in general, the economics of local news, is something that we really just need to learn more about.

Matt Grossmann: There's a lot more to learn. The science of politics is available biweekly from the Niskanen Center and part of the Democracy Group Network. I'm your host, Matt Grossman.

VIEWPOINT 4

> "With such a highly concentrated media ownership, the partisanship of big news brands has become the norm."

Why We Need Media Diversity

Tim Dwyer

In this viewpoint Tim Dwyer discusses a case in which the misuse of media for corporate interests in Australia became evident. In this case, a media magnate named Kerry Stokes used the media company he owns—Seven West Media—to attack a competitor in the mining equipment industry with the clear purpose of negatively impacting the competition's business. What makes this even more troubling is that Seven West Media owns the only major newspaper in Perth, a major Australian city, demonstrating a clear lack of media diversity. When there are fewer news sources available, bias and misinformation are more likely to take hold. Dwyer turns to a new regulatory framework in the EU to provide an example for how to protect media diversity. Tim Dwyer is an associate professor of media and communications at the University of Sydney in Australia.

"Billionaire Stoush over Alleged Media Bias Highlights the Need for Greater Media Diversity," by Tim Dwyer, February 23, 2023, https://theconversation.com/billionaire-stoush-over-alleged-media-bias-highlights-the-need-for-greater-media-diversity-200354. Licensed under CC BY-ND 4.0 International.

Does Media Consolidation Increase Misinformation, Bias, and Polarization?

As you read, consider the following questions:

1. What does the Australian Senate mean when it says Australia's media regulation is a "system not fit-for-purpose"? What examples are provided?
2. What is the European Media Freedom Act (EMFA) meant to accomplish?
3. What changes are being made to the way the Australian Communications and Media Authority (ACMA) measures media diversity?

The recent stoush between mining magnate Andrew "Twiggy" Forrest and media mogul Kerry Stokes is just the latest flashing neon sign above the parlous state of media diversity in Australia.

Laws protecting media diversity in Australia have been gradually dismantled in recent decades. Because of this, their objective of preventing a select few media owners or voices from having too much influence over public opinion and the political agenda has been placed at risk.

But traditional approaches to protecting media diversity may be less effective as the role of online news – now curated for us using algorithms – becomes ever more prominent in our news diets. This could require a new approach.

Misuse of Media Power?

Stokes' Seven West Media owns the West Australian Newspaper, the only major daily paper in Perth. Stokes also has a controlling interest in the mining equipment company WesTrac, which supplies Caterpillar mining machinery.

Forrest's Fortescue Metals previously had a supply arrangement with WesTrac. But he then placed on order to purchase 120 emission-free, hauling trucks from the German Liebherr company, putting him in direct competition with WesTrac.

Forrest claims this move was met with "biased, inflammatory and inaccurate" coverage about his company in Seven West Media.

Media Consolidation

In a complaint to Communications Minister Michelle Rowland, Mark Hutchinson, the chief executive of Fortescue Future Industries, described what he calls "the misuse of the West Australian newspaper to pursue commercial interests". He added, according to the ABC:

> The West's coverage has gone far beyond fair scrutiny and is clearly driven by fossil fuel interests with the aim of damaging Fortescue's green energy mission.

"System Not Fit-for-Purpose"

Hutchinson says the issues points to a wider problem: the lack of media diversity in Perth, which has only one major daily newspaper for a city of two million.

That Seven West Media is one of only three major commercial corporations owning the bulk of Australian media – alongside News Corp and Nine Entertainment – is a sad indictment of the state of our media ownership laws.

With such a highly concentrated media ownership, the partisanship of big news brands has become the norm. The Senate inquiry into media diversity has investigated a litany of problems associated with this, deeming Australian media regulation a "system not fit-for-purpose".

For example, Australia's relationship with China, its largest trading partner, is typically cast in hyperbolic "war drums" language by the Murdoch media. And during the pandemic, News Corp's online tabloids were especially keen to link COVID with China. China scholar David Brophy documented in his book, *China Panic*, how Sky News seized on a "dodgy-dossier" linking COVID to a laboratory in the city of Wuhan.

More recently, News Corp is at it again, this time airing an hour-long special advocating for a doubling of Australia's military spending so the country can be protected against the imminent and "inevitable" Chinese invasion.

In its final report, the media diversity inquiry commented,

It is noteworthy that the overwhelming majority of the evidence to this inquiry relates to one dominant media organization, News Corp.

How Europe Is Leading the Way

To counter unaccountable media power and a lack of transparency in media ownership, the European Commission has recently proposed a new regulatory framework: the European Media Freedom Act (EMFA).

Introducing the new framework, EU commissioner Thierry Breton said it contains

> [...]common safeguards at EU level to guarantee a plurality of voices and that our media are able to operate without any interference, be it private or public.

He said a new European watchdog would be set up to ensure transparency in media ownership. Another key feature will require EU member states to test the impact of media market concentrations on media pluralism and editorial independence.

At a recent EU parliament hearing, a media freedom expert, Elda Brogi, explained how the new measures benefit the public as well as regulators:

> [...] it helps media users to understand how ownership may influence the [news] content.

A Better Method for Measuring Media Diversity

The Australian government and its principal media regulator, the Australian Communications and Media Authority (ACMA), have recently released a discussion paper seeking comment on developing a sophisticated new way to monitor media diversity in Australia.

This is the second phase of a process begun in 2020. The goal is to assess how Australians actually consume online news, including personalised news delivered to them through social media, search engines and news aggregators.

Media Consolidation

The current media diversity rules are based on an assessment of the ownership and control of traditional media outlets. However, as ACMA says, this misses the volume of news being published and consumed online. This omission is "notable", the agency says, given 81% of Australians access news content online.

This news measurement model will be able to track the level of connection of stories (news connected to localities), the extent of originality (unique news stories), and the level of civic journalism (news of public significance).

This kind of internationally informed and evidenced-based approach is urgently needed to truly gauge the level of media concentration in Australia and determine its impact on public interest journalism and the news people read. Only then can we put in place new regulations that will have a real impact.

Periodical and Internet Sources Bibliography

The following articles have been selected to supplement the diverse views presented in this chapter.

Luke Auburn, "Study of Headlines Shows Media Bias Is Growing," University of Rochester News Center, July 13, 2023. https://www.rochester.edu/newscenter/study-of-headlines-shows-media-bias-growing-563502/.

Joe Berkowitz, "Why Worker-Owned Publications like Defector and 404 Media Are Winning," Fast Company, November 19, 2023. https://www.fastcompany.com/90983739/worker-owned-media-future-defector-aftermath-404.

Ronan Farrow, "Elon Musk's Shadow Rule," *New Yorker*, August 21, 2023. https://www.newyorker.com/magazine/2023/08/28/elon-musks-shadow-rule.

Ashley Johnson, "New Evidence Shows Blaming Social Media for Political Polarization Is Misguided," Information and Technology Innovation Foundation, August 8, 2023. https://itif.org/publications/2023/08/08/new-evidence-shows-blaming-social-media-for-political-polarization-is-misguided/.

Nickie Louise, "These 6 Corporations Control 90% of the Media Outlets in America. The Illusion of Choice and Objectivity," Tech Startups, September 18, 2020. https://techstartups.com/2020/09/18/6-corporations-control-90-media-america-illusion-choice-objectivity-2020/.

Benjamin Mullin and Katie Robertson, "A Decade Ago, Jeff Bezos Bought a Newspaper. Now He's Paying Attention to It Again," *New York Times*, July 22, 2023. https://www.nytimes.com/2023/07/22/business/media/jeff-bezos-washington-post.html.

Joe Pompeo, "Once Renegade Vice Anxiously Awaits Its Private Equity Overlords," *Vanity Fair*, May 19, 2023. https://www.vanityfair.com/news/2023/05/vice-media-bankruptcy-sale.

Katia Savchuk, "A Surprising Discovery About Facebook's Role in Driving Polarization," Stanford Graduate School of Business, September 14, 2023. https://www.gsb.stanford.edu/insights/surprising-discovery-about-facebooks-role-driving-polarization.

Media Consolidation

Ari Shapiro, Michael Levitt, and Christopher Intagliata, "How the Polarizing Effect of Social Media Is Speeding Up," NPR, September 9, 2022. https://www.npr.org/2022/09/09/1121295499/facebook-twitter-youtube-instagram-tiktok-social-media.

Charlie Warzel, "Elon Musk Is a Far-Right Activist," *The Atlantic*, December 11, 2022. https://www.theatlantic.com/technology/archive/2022/12/elon-musk-twitter-far-right-activist/672436/.

For Further Discussion

Chapter 1

1. Based on what you've read in this chapter, what do you think is the value of independent journalism? Are those benefits tangible or intangible? How do they compare to the benefits of corporate media?
2. In this chapter we learned details about the media habits of people who are actively engaged in their local communities. What do you think is the relationship between being active in local politics and keeping up with politics at the national level? How important do you think local news is to a vibrant democracy?
3. In one viewpoint in this chapter, the authors point out that media-bashing corporations have contributed to a lack of trust in media. Why do you think some corporations would want to decrease the trust in media?

Chapter 2

1. In her interview with Lucas Shaw in this chapter, Terry Gross says that the media "just becomes about making profit and, you know, beating out the competition. So some things that are really valuable can't just be measured in profit and in measuring yourself against the metrics of other companies." Do you agree with this statement in relation to media? Explain your answer.
2. Based on what you've read in this chapter, do you think that the problems posed by corporate consolidation might be mitigated by more and stronger unions? Why or why not?
3. In the viewpoint by Mark Poepsel, the author talks about how mass media and communication have changed over time. Do you think the current shift could reduce the cultural power and reach of media conglomerates? Why or why not?

Media Consolidation

Chapter 3

1. The viewpoint by Margot Susca in this chapter refers to a time when news programming was not intended to be profitable, but to meet the requirement that media companies provide a public service in order to be permitted to use common airwaves, airwaves that are publicly owned. How has the news changed since news divisions became profit motivated?

2. In his viewpoint, Tejvan Pettinger argues that monopolies can have some advantages, at least at the product level. These include lower prices and more product variety. In your opinion, do monopolies such as Amazon (which sells books) and media companies that sell movies, video games, or internet access offer advantages to the consumer? If so, what are those advantages?

3. The United States first began breaking up monopolies around the beginning of the 20th century. How have policies changed since then to allow for an increase in monopolies in the 21st century?

Chapter 4

1. In this chapter, there are contrasting viewpoints on whether media consolidation increases political bias. What are some points supporting this idea? What are some points that suggest consolidation hasn't increased bias? What is your opinion?

2. According to the viewpoints in this chapter, how can journalists and politicians fight political bias in the age of media consolidation?

3. Based on what you've read in the viewpoints in this chapter, what are the political impacts of having fewer news sources available to the public?

| 166

Organizations to Contact

The editors have compiled the following list of organizations concerned with the issues debated in this book. The descriptions are derived from materials provided by the organizations. All have publications or information available for interested readers. The list was compiled on the date of publication of the present volume; the information provided here may change. Be aware that many organizations take several weeks or longer to respond to inquiries, so allow as much time as possible.

Institute for Nonprofit News (INN)

8549 Wilshire Boulevard, #2294
Beverly Hills, CA 90211
(818) 582-3560
email: info@inn.org
website: https://inn.org

INN is a nonprofit news network that works to ensure all communities have access to trusted news. The organization provides education and business support services to member organizations and promotes the value and benefit of public-service and investigative journalism.

International Federation of Journalists (IFJ)

PC-Residence Palace, Bloc C
Rue de la Loi 155
B-1040 Brussels
Belgium
32 (0)2 235 22 00
email: ifj@ifj.org
website: www.ifj.org

Nearly a century old, the IFJ is an organization that represents almost 600,000 journalists and media professionals, supporting fair

167 |

Media Consolidation

pay, gender equity, and strong unions for journalists. It works to support journalists and the freedom of the press around the world.

National Association of Black Journalists (NABJ)

1100 Knight Hall, Suite 3101
College Park, MD 20742
(301) 405-0248
email: contact@nabj.org
website: https://nabjonline.org

Since 1975, the NABJ has offered professional development and training for Black journalists, journalism students, and media professionals throughout the United States. It offers training, information about media job opportunities, and scholarship and internship opportunities to its members, among other resources.

National Association of Science Writers (NASW)

PO Box 7905
Berkeley, CA 94707
(510) 859-7229
website: www.nasw.org
email: director@nasw.org

NASW was founded in 1934 and works to support effective science journalism by providing its members opportunities with helpful resources and access to scientific journals. It works to promote the free flow of science news through press freedoms, which can help combat misinformation.

National Scholastic Press Association (NSPA)

2829 University Avenue SE, Suite 720
Minneapolis, MN 55414
(612) 200-9254
email: info@studentpress.org
website: www.studentpress.org/nspa

The NSPA provides educational benefits and resources to students, teachers, and media advisors. Based in Minneapolis and with over 1,500 member publications, the organization has a worldwide influence on the journalism profession.

Nieman Foundation

Walter Lippmann House
One Francis Avenue
Cambridge, MA 02138
(617) 495-2237
website: https:// nieman.harvard.edu

Nieman Foundation is an organization based at Harvard University dedicated to promoting and elevating the standards of journalism by educating and supporting, often through fellowships, those poised to make important contributions to the future of journalism. It also offers online and print publications offering reporting on media.

The Poynter Institute

801 Third Street South
St. Petersburg, FL 33701
(727) 821-9494
email: info@poynter.org
website: www.poynter.org

The Poynter Institute is a nonprofit journalism school and research organization that serves as a resource for individuals and organizations that aspire to engage and inform citizens. It is dedicated to strengthening the role of journalism in a free society and protecting freedom of the press.

Media Consolidation

Society of Environmental Journalists (SEJ)

1629 K Street NW, Suite 300
Washington, DC 20006
(202) 558-2055
email: sej@sej.org
website: www.sej.org

The SEJ assists journalists covering environmental issues, in part by uniting scientists and journalists. The organization also works to raise awareness among key stakeholders, editors, publishers, and news managers of the importance of environmental news reporting.

Society of Professional Journalists (SPJ)

P.O. Box 441748
Indianapolis, IN 46244
(317) 927-8000
website: www.spj.org

The SPJ supports journalists at every state of their careers through various programs and competitions. Recently the organization has begun a collaboration with Google to inspire a positive influence with journalism in the newsroom and classroom.

World Association of News Publishers (WAN-IFRA)

Rotfeder-Ring 11
60327 Frankfurt
Germany
49 69 2400630
email: info@wan-ifra.org
website: https://wan-ifra.org

A global network that has been around since 1948, WAN-IFRA is dedicated to protecting free press and journalism around the world. It advocates for press freedom, supports equity in the news industry, and works to protect independent journalism.

Bibliography of Books

Giles Clark and Angus Phillips. *Inside Book Publishing*. 6th ed. Oxford, UK: Routledge, 2020.

David Dayen. *Monopolized: Life in the Age of Corporate Power*. New York, NY: The New Press, 2020.

J. Bradford DeLong. *Slouching Towards Utopia: An Economic History of the Twentieth Century*. New York, NY: Basic, 2022.

Kent Greenfield. *Corporations Are People Too (And They Should Act Like It)*. New Haven, CT: Yale University Press, 2018.

Edward S. Herman and Noam Chomsky. *Manufacturing Consent: The Political Economy of the Mass Media*. Reprint ed. New York, NY: Pantheon, 2002.

Brooke Kroeger. *Undaunted: How Women Changed American Journalism*. New York, NY: Random House, 2023.

William Magnuson. *For Profit: A History of Corporations*. New York, NY: Basic, 2022.

Naomi Oreskes and Erik M. Conway. *The Big Myth: How American Business Taught Us to Loathe Government and Love the Free Market*. New York, NY: Bloomsbury, 2023.

Ingrid Robeyns. *Limitarianism: The Case Against Extreme Wealth*. New York, NY: Astra House, 2024.

Michael Shudson. *Journalism: Why It Matters*. Cambridge, UK: Polity Press, 2020.

Dan Sinykin. *Big Fiction: How Conglomeration Changed the Publishing Industry and American Literature*. New York, NY: Columbia University Press, 2023.

Matt Stoller. *Goliath: The 100-Year War Between Monopoly Power and Democracy*. New York, NY: Simon and Schuster, 2019.

Media Consolidation

Zephyr Teachout. *Break 'Em Up: Recovering Our Freedom from Big Ag, Big Tech, and Big Money.* New York, NY: All Points Books, 2020.

Andie Tucher. *Not Exactly Lying: Fake News and Fake Journalism in American History.* New York, NY: Columbia University Press, 2022.

Adam Winkler. *We the Corporations: How American Businesses Won Their Civil Rights.* New York, NY: Liveright, 2018.

Marin Wolf. *The Crisis of Democratic Capitalism.* New York, NY: Penguin, 2023.

Index

A

Amazon, 91, 104, 105, 119
  monopoly of, 110–111
antitrust laws, 15, 51, 105–106, 107
artificial intelligence, use of by
  companies, 70–76

B

bias, 15, 16, 32, 37, 80, 83, 91, 124,
  125–128, 131, 156, 158, 159
book publishing,
  digital, 15, 57, 64, 66–69
  Internet Archive and, 67
  small and medium-sized
    publishers, 64–69

C

cable television, 58, 60–62
censorship, 31–37
children, advertising and, 50
Citizens United decision, 40, 112
Clinton, Bill, 14, 97, 100
competition, lack/reduction of, 18,
  61, 97, 153
convergence, 77, 84–85
corporations
  control of access to information
    and, 48–53
  media houses and, 22–23
  shaping politics, 38–43
COVID-19, 33

culture, effect of media
  consolidation on, 15, 57–92

D

democracy and media
  consolidation, 14, 15, 18–53,
  57, 99
deregulation of media, 14–15, 97,
  100–103
Disney, 48–53, 61, 62, 63

E

economic results of media
  consolidation, 15, 96–120
equal time, giving to all sides, 14

F

Fairness Doctrine, 14
fake news, 128, 132–133
Federal Communications
  Commission (FCC), 14, 47, 98,
  99–103, 110–111, 124, 129, 133,
  138, 150, 154
First Amendment, 31, 33
free press, 18, 45

I

independent media and reporting,
  34–35, 37

173

Media Consolidation

J

January 6 insurrection, 32

job losses, 15, 59, 71, 74, 101, 102

journalists, hostility toward, 29

L

local news coverage, 15, 99, 102

civic engagement and, 18, 19–24

decrease in, 15, 124, 125–128, 130–134, 136, 137–138, 141, 142–144, 151–152

nationalization of, 135–157

M

main studio rule, 99–100, 102, 124, 150, 154

mass media's impact on culture, 77–88

media diversity, need for, 158–162

misinformation, 16, 29, 44–47, 124, 158

money/profits made by media consolidation, 23, 42–43, 50, 62, 70, 97–103, 109–113, 150–151

monopolies, advantages and disadvantages of, 104–107, 115–120

Murdoch, Rupert, 22, 51, 61, 160

N

Netflix, 49, 62, 89–92

news broadcasters/divisions

based in local communities, 15, 99, 102

distortion of news, 31–37

as profit centers, 97–103

News Corp, 22, 51, 160

O

opposing viewpoints, importance of, 11–13

P

Paramount Global, 61–62

polarization, 16, 28, 130, 135–157

politics and the media, 28, 29, 37, 38–43, 135–157

Project Censored, 31–37

R

Reagan, Ronald, 14

regulations on media, 14, 98

S

Sinclair Broadcast Group, 109, 112–113, 125–128, 129–134, 136, 137, 139–140, 150–151, 152–153, 154–155

social media, 27, 32, 57, 76, 77, 81, 82, 117, 124, 132–133

statistics on media consolidation, 15, 51

streaming services, 57, 60–61, 63, 91

strike, writers' and actors', 15, 58, 59, 70, 72–73, 75

T

Telecommunications Act of 1996, 14, 97, 100, 102

Index

television and film industries, effects of media consolidation on, 58–63, 108–114

Time Warner, 22, 60, 101

trust in the media, 18, 25–30

21st Century Fox, 48–53, 101

W

Warner Bros. Discovery, 60, 63

Y

YouTube, 36, 37, 59, 77, 81, 85, 86

Media Consolidation